I WILL NOT FEAR

*Walking in Greater Wholeness and Victory
by Defeating Anxiety, Stress and Worry*

Mark DeJesus

I Will Not Fear
Walking in Greater Wholeness and Victory by Defeating Anxiety, Stress and Worry
By Mark T. DeJesus
Turning Hearts Ministries
www.markdejesus.com
Copyright 2008 – Mark DeJesus

Published By: Mark DeJesus and Lulu.com

ISBN 13: 978-0-6152-2042-0

Cover Design By: Michael Henin of christiancollages.com

Contents

Dedication and Acknowledgements

I love you God, because you first loved me. With a grateful heart, I give eternal thanks to my Heavenly Father, who loves me so infinitely and continually reveals His love and plans for me. I am glad that I can call you Dad. I want to thank you Jesus for being my Redeemer and the Way to the Father. Thank you for showing me the perfect model of the Christian life. Holy Spirit, you are an eternal comfort and guide. You empower and lead me to speak and do what comes from the Father.

I would not be the man I am today without my wife Melissa. God divinely brought you into my life and through you I have understood love in a way I had never experienced. You are my greatest encourager. Because of your belief in who God made me to be, I have been able to face tremendous obstacles and fears to pursue all that God has for me to do. I am honored to have you as my wife, best friend, lover and ministry partner.

I want to thank my parents for giving me a rich spiritual heritage in the things of God. I credit your labors to the early encounters I experienced with God. Your testimony and hunger for God's truth have encouraged me to find answers for struggles I face in God's Word.

I want to thank an ever growing list of friends, mentors and fellow laborers who have made tremendous impacts on my life and helped aim me towards my personal destiny.

To those who need a breakthrough in any area of fear: *this book is for you.* If this writing project is a blessing in any way, helping you to walk through fear and stir up your divine destiny, then my breakthrough was worth it. This book is also dedicated to all those who will make the decision to join the fight against fear and change generations to come.

Introduction

Men's hearts failing them for fear . . .
Luke 21:26

In these days, fear is spreading throughout all the earth in various forms, bringing emotional, mental and physical despair to all of mankind like never before. Whether it is anxiety, phobias, panic attacks, worry or timidity, the goal is still the same: steal, kill and destroy. This underground torment is plaguing our families, communities, churches and fellowships in massive assaults. As a result of fear's attacks, people are showing increasing signs of mental unrest and even physical disease.

It has been placed deeply on my heart to attack this problem of fear at a higher level because it is affecting humanity both outside the church and within. The cry of those who are bound and sick is too loud for me to ignore anymore. Because of this, I have been profoundly stirred to unveil the mission of fear: to rob mankind of peace, security and courage. It is depriving people of being able to give and receive love, which is desperately needed in this hour to heal broken hearts and deliver a vision of God's perfecting purpose into lives. Brothers and sisters have lost their sense of rest and are unable to hear God's voice clearly because they have been bound by fear's arsenal: anxiety, phobias, stress and worry.

Because of fear's workings, men's hearts are failing; in passion, vision and even physical health. Stress is moving upon our nation to the point that people have become emotionally and physically limited and even diseased, while others are desperately seeking relief from depression and anxiety disorders. As a result, many are losing hope in God and are turning to man made resources for answers: doctors, psychologists and even new age practitioners. Yet in the hearts of people is a cry that says, "There must be a better way."

In my 25 year journey as a Christian, it has amazed me that Christian believers struggle with just as much anxiety and worry as those who were unbelievers, with little improvement. I myself also came under its grip for quite some time, which sent me on a journey to find true and solid answers from God to set me free. In these pages, not only will you uncover some answers to your fear struggles, you will also find the conclusions and even revelations I obtained after years of diligent study, prayer, and godly mentoring.

I ask you to read this book with an open heart, because there is a move of the Holy Spirit, coming from the very heart of Father God to set people free in the name of His Son Jesus. His heart's desire is to touch your heart, so I encourage you to open it up to Him. Ask Him to help you keep yourself tender towards Him so He can begin to do a cleansing and healing work in your life. You may be reading this book for yourself or for someone that you know who struggles with fear issues, needs emotional healing or desperately needs a physical healing. Keep an open heart so that God can deliver His love and power.

The truth is that God has possessed an eternal desire to work in and through the *hearts* of people. Yet it is the hearts of mankind that are broken and confused by the attacks of fear, thus making it challenging to perceive and receive the love and goodness of God. Often times, the very thing that God wants to touch and use for His eternal purposes (our hearts) has been contaminated by the continual attacks of fear. Yet in His divine plan of freedom, God is moving mightily to touch the hearts of people and bring a restoration of His love that will lead them away from fear and into faith in Him.

This divine mission of touching the hearts of mankind and setting people free was reiterated when Jesus declared His purpose in Luke 4.

The Spirit of the Lord is upon me, because he hath anointed me to preach the gospel to the poor; he hath sent me to heal the brokenhearted, to preach deliverance to the captives, and recovering of sight to the blind, to set at liberty them that are bruised, to preach the acceptable year of the Lord.
Luke 4:18-19

The message I am delivering is one of love and freedom. I firmly believe that fear has dominated our lives and our thoughts for too long. It is robbing us of our sanity and health and the time has come to put a stop to it. Walking into freedom over fear is going to manifest as clusters of brothers and sisters make decisions to march towards victory and make a declaration that they will no longer tolerate fear in their lives any longer.

As an encouragement, I want you to know that those who struggle with any area of fear are not crazy and are also not alone. You may have thought processes and patterns of fear that have been in existence since birth, but you can make a change to be free. There are also others who may not think they struggle with fear related issues, yet the Lord could use this book to help bring an illumination, giving you an opportunity to walk towards victory. Others may be serving fear in many ways, but have justified it as normal living. Today you can begin to say, "God I want to take a new step," and on the authority of what the Bible says, you can walk towards wholeness.

I encourage you to carefully read this book from beginning to end, because within these chapters there is a progressive flow of teaching. Let the God speak to your heart as you read and allow His ways to become alive within you. The power of God's truth can bring healing and deliverance even as you read and receive what is in these pages. This is an opportunity for you to begin a journey that will lead you into God's love in ways that you have never experienced before.

Our Heavenly Father wants to set His children free from fear and the effects it has put on their mind, health and relationships. This message is a timely one that will have earth shattering effects on communities that apply it. God's desire is to free us so we can help free others.

I am so excited that you are taking this step. May God bless you as we pursue this journey together.

Section I

The Reality of Fear's Effects

Chapter 1

What Is There To Be Afraid Of?

Fear is everywhere! Turn on the television or view any form of popular media and you will quickly observe fearful expressions far and wide. As you watch and listen to world-wide communication, you will interestingly notice that fear has an ability to draw in the attention of an audience in many ways. In fact, fear-driven media communication can even bolster television ratings. Often you will find news stations preying off the anxieties and worries that people have by magnifying them or by inventing new ones. Next time you turn on the news, take careful notice as the broadcasts will use fear tactics to suck the audience into staying tuned for the rest of the broadcast. You'll hear preview clips that say, "Tune in to the 11 o'clock news and find out why your children are not safe in your neighborhood. Live at 6; find out what is on your kitchen counter that could be killing you." It is a pathetic attempt to attract more viewers, but the fact is most of the time, it works pretty effectively.

The Effects of Terrorism

Since September 11, 2001, the United States and even much of the world has had a greater vulnerability to fear as tragedy suddenly came upon the American homeland. A great deal of panic and anxiety began to spread rapidly when our safety and security seemed to become compromised. Even though we have experienced tremendous amounts of safety in this land, a vast amount of fear came upon our people as a result of that traumatic day. Over time, America has experienced some healing from these fear-filled attacks, but many are still very apprehensive and anxious over the threat of future attacks.

Terrorism is a severe concern for many around the world. By definition, terrorism is "the systematic use of terror especially as a means of coercion[1]." In other words, terrorism uses anxiety and panic to manipulate and oppress people and nations. The work of terrorism certainly conveys the power that fear can have over people. Often the fearful anticipation of potential attack can be terrorism's greatest threat.

In an article from the Washington Post, survey results were posted as to the American sentiment regarding feelings of safety and their overall outlook towards the threat on American security. Fewer than half of all Americans in this survey thought the country is safer now than it was on Sept. 11, 2001, and more than three-quarters expected the United States to be the target of a major terrorist attack at home or abroad in the next few months. The survey also found that about half of those who responded were concerned that terrorists would strike near their home or work. Seventy-three percent communicated in this survey that they were anxious or concerned about terrorism, and a small percentage, 26 percent claimed that they were calm[2].

Marketing Strategies

Fear can be found in abundance when it comes to the business arena and marketing, mainly because magnified fear can actually increase economic consumption. Businesses can fall prey to using fear in order to sell items and improve their marketing draw. In fact, some even use a technique called the *Fear, Uncertainty and Doubt* (or FUD) strategy. This strategy is executed when a sales person or a business as a whole attempts to stir up *fear* in a potential customer by first addressing an issue that presents danger and discomfort. The highlighted matter may not be that perilous or threatening at all, but a clear effort is made to raise concern. The FUD strategy stirs up a "need" within in you for their product, even if that need was not in existence prior to this sales attempt. Their product is then fabulously presented as a "solution" to the "problem at hand". The sales team will then emphasize an *uncertainty* of what could happen if you do not buy and use their product, or if you try and "settle" for the competitor's product. Lastly, they will also feed you with *doubt*, leading you to question why one would even bother using the competitor's product. This process is meant to intensely motivate an audience, market a product and bring in massive sales. This seems like a sly attempt; but one that profits businesses by the billions.

Performance Pressure

As we can see in countries across the world, the more a nation becomes industrialized, the more intense the competitive pressures arise for that society to *produce* and to *perform* at high levels. With that pressure comes a tremendous opening for fear, stress, anxiety and worry to factor in at epidemic proportions. You may even notice this intense trend spreading in your own work place. Regrettably, we are observing the staggering results of stress in our country already. In our culture you will find fear, stress, worry and anxiety in occurrence so often that people seem to look at them as positive entities. They have become so familiar that most cannot understand life without that pressure. If someone is not experiencing major stress and fear pressures, they are sometimes seen as lazy or "not with it" in today's culture. Those who are intensely overstressed and overloaded are often admired as being hard working and wise.

Stress can easily open the door and enter in because of our predisposition towards always needing to be busy. With that constant busyness comes a pressure to perform and achieve. Even more disturbing is the inability to maintain personal peace or quiet confidence because of all the chaos. The reality is that the stress, noise, and constant movement seem to be incredibly productive in the short term, yet over the long haul the destructive consequences will manifest.

Over the years, the standards of performance and bottom line results are raised higher. At the same time, levels of stress and tension increase right along with it. Yet instead of making significant changes and creating healthy boundaries and expectations, we feast for more because we have been so deeply programmed to drive hard in remaining extremely competitive. As a result, because we maintain this "drive and perform at all costs" mentality, our well-being is suffering.

Fear-Filled Entertainment

It is amazing to observe the fascination and oftentimes strange delight that humans have for leisure activities that are intentionally induced with fear. Millions of folks all over the world gather in entertainment venues of varied formats to observe storylines and performances that stimulate all kinds of fearful reactions. Action and suspense movies are called "thrillers" because of their ability to bring flashes of exhilaration through the portrayal of fearful situations. This brings excitement to audiences because of their thirst to experience a crisis or a moment of sheer adrenaline rush. Although this entertainment can be enjoyable and exciting (especially for those that lack excitement in their lives), many movie studios take fear to a whole different level.

Horror movie producers step in and visually craft all kinds of terrifying situations by unleashing unthinkable situations of gore and fright onto a screen. You would think that most people would not want to pay money to be frightened or induced to anxiousness. Yet the popular response is always overwhelming as people pay to see more. As of this writing, there are even some very popular web sites popping up that are solely based on promoting fearful movies that have horror and terror as their theme. Their theme is *the scarier the better*.

Video games are right alongside the movie industry in pushing the envelope to gain more attention through edgier and more intense games. Through casual observation, one can see that the more blood and the more action that is offered, the better the sales of games. Roller coasters are seen in just about every amusement park, and rides are driven to push human emotions to greater reaction and higher suspense. The element of surprise is intensified as technology has enhanced the abilities of companies to produce rides that are scarier and more intense[3].

Scientists and researchers have tried to identify the reason for this strange fascination that people have with frightening entertainment. Although many studies have been done and continual experiments will be attempted, very little information comes forth to bring solid scientific reasoning for this attraction and behavior. Yet one thing is very certain: *human beings seem to be addicted to the rush that a fearful thrill brings them.* The normal adrenaline used in genuinely "fearful" situations actually feels pleasurable to entertainment seekers because their mind preserves the outlook that they are safe and not experiencing anything truly harmful. Also, this kind of entertainment is an obvious escape from the realities of life and it helps in relieving some of their own personal pain. What seems to make engaging in this type of entertainment so much more pleasurable is the idea that what they are watching or experiencing is not real and will end soon. Yet many times the effects of this can be damaging[4].

Family Fear

On a note more close to home, many families are plagued with a significant amount of fear that lurks in their home which manifests itself in countless ways. Homes filled with constant arguing and strife can stir up an atmosphere that lacks love and security; thus creating an avenue for fear to become a predator. Additionally, traumatic experiences in home life can lock in fearful associations when children or spouses are abused physically, verbally, or sexually. A pressure in the home to perform and excel at extremely high standards can lead to a heavy sense of drivenness and perfectionism in our children. This can drive them to the point that the fear of failure becomes their number one dread while being their leading motivator all at once. In this situation, failure of any kind produces emotional wounding in a child's mind as they learn that mistakes are frowned upon. This increases the potential for fear to seep in as kids do not feel safe and loved.

This doesn't just apply to children either. Similar oppression can be placed on any adult just as easily. Where there is a lack of love in a family, there is more room for fear to operate. Since this is not always addressed effectively and lovingly in family trees, various forms of fear issues end up being repeated, generation after generation.

Today's teenagers face an onslaught of fear and intimidation that much of the world has never seen before. Young people in this time encounter hours of constant peer-pressures, which manifest in various manners and forms. With great influence, fear comes in to pressure teens into behaving a certain way and conforming to a particular image. Because many teens are in an awkward stage of insecurity and in many cases do not experience loving environments at home, the temptation to give in to these pressures increases. Those who are vulnerable to peer-pressure will do anything to get accepted. The threat of not being received into a group becomes a major threat to their confidence. The fear of rejection can be a driving force throughout their lives, causing them to make horrible decisions. In addition, the temptation to indulge in sexual activity, drug use, and rebellious behavior become more of a reality when the fear of other people and the fear of rejection are on the scene. These fears can cripple a young person's self-confidence and can last well into the adult years.

Years ago I spent more than 7 years as a youth pastor, and had the responsibility to connect with hundreds of teenagers and families. As I got to know the families in the church, I observed that the parents deeply struggled to connect with their children, and did not know how to authentically maneuver through the changes in their teens' life. For many of these sincere parents, I felt compassion for them because I knew that they were not shown love and nurturing in their own households growing up. They were raised by parents who were strict, unloving and cold. As a result, they walked into parenting with their own brokenness still intact and no references on how to lovingly raise a child in the nurture and admonition of the Lord. The outcome was that the unresolved damage of their past affected how they dealt with their own teenage children. Their dysfunction and inability to connect with their kids opened the way for intimidation and control to become the chosen methods motivation. Many times this led to a family run by rules without relationship, which undoubtedly can lead to rebellion. This ultimately repeated the patterns of their parents which they sincerely thought would never happen.

In the early childhood years, fear can take root and carry on into adult life. Many people in their mid-life years begin to manifest the pain and dysfunction that their childhood fears brought on. Yet they do not even realize how or where it began. Many are able to manage through their twenties, but once in their thirties and forties, symptoms begin to manifest, which we will cover later in this book. Yet at the source of many of their struggles is most likely a root of fear that has never been dealt with. As I will explain in further chapters, because these matters are not tackled, mental health and disease become a greater part of our society. When fear has not been properly addressed and resolved, the results can be devastating.

Pressure Tactics

Unfortunately people can even attempt to use fear as their own tool for motivation, which ends up really becoming *manipulation*. Because fear can have such a powerful effect on us, it can be very easy for bosses or leaders to send signals of intimidation with the masked intention to "motivate" or "inspire" employees or subordinates into action. The intention may be a fine one, but the methods are backed with fear and dysfunction. Many times in corporations, proper vision casting, kindness and communication with care are not being practiced in healthy fashion, which leads to poor productivity and weak progress. When this happens, the easy route is taken as superiors resort to motivating with fear as their game plan. Unfortunately, in many cases this can bring added productivity so the pressure tactics seem to be "successful." Yet spiritually and emotionally, they are mechanisms that create bondage for both the one who intimidates and the one receiving the manipulation and intimidation. The Scriptures teach us that the fear of man brings a snare[5] and this snare will catch all those involved into a trap if they are not wise and aware.

A Widespread Effect

Community groups, political arenas and even churches are no strangers to these dangerous pressure tactics of fear. In fact, many times it runs at a much higher octane in these venues. Political and social communities use intimidation as a regular method to reel in control that leaders feel they need to have to thrust their agenda. It's in these atmospheres that fear steps in and pressures people to gain control by intimidating those who stand in their way.

Churches are no strangers to fear pressures at all. Unfortunately, you will find fear operating in both small and large churches all across the world. Authority structures and committees battle in power struggles while using position or power to intimidate people into subjection and conformity. Although many times done in the name of success, improvement, motivation, and even the name of Jesus, in simplest terms these tools are really just manipulation. In all honesty, people should never be led and guided by intimidation and manipulation. This should never be used over people and it should never be sat under. Yet many respond affirmatively to these tactics because of the fear of being rejected by man and even God. The problem is that it is robbing people of freedom, and unfortunately for those who fall under this influence, the long term results can be painful and devastating.

Worry Words

In our verbal communication, we can send signals that can seriously induce fear in ourselves and others. By simply using the right words, we can send shockwaves of fear to someone that can discourage and dampen their development. Although well meaning, people can spew out words of constant fear rather than encouraging faith. In many cases what happens when we speak fear-ridden words is that we speak out of our *own* fears and traumas. As a result, we do not allow words of faith, love and hope to invade our discussions.

The real truth is that fear manifests itself in so much of our language and expressions. I run into people almost on a daily basis whose words are predominantly tainted with the vocabulary of fear. Phrases like, "What if?" and "I hope this doesn't go wrong" and "this isn't going to work out" become regular ways of talking. If you stop and think about the way you speak and the way your words project fear into the future, you will start to realize: my talk is loaded with fear. It becomes a driving force in too many of the thoughts, words and actions that take place in society. When fear enters the scene, atmospheres that should be havens of safety, love, comfort and acceptance are contaminated with fear, torment and anxiousness. There is no question. Fear has had a major influence in society and must be dealt with.

The Vocabulary of Fear

In the English language, there are a number of words used to express the different facets and expressions of fear. A casual mental exercise will bring quite a few of them to mind along with mental references. An interesting discovery is made when we see the definitions and origins behind many of the expressions of fear that we throw around. This will help our journey to overcome what fear has done in our lives. The findings may actually surprise you.

Worry

We use the term *worry* in our modern day culture as a way to describe how we concern ourselves for the future. It causes us to be troubled over an issue and to feel uneasy about an upcoming event. Worry tends to leave things unresolved within us and causes people to lack peace about the future. This word describes how we mull over things and ponder continually about issues and events that deeply concern us. For most people, it can be a temporary thing, but in many cases it can become chronic. The interesting thing is that the middle age English word definition for worry (which is where this word comes from) means "to strangle, choke, or constrict, to harass by tearing, biting, or snapping especially at the throat". It also means "to feel or experience concern or anxiety[6]."

Anxiety

Merriam-Webster's Dictionary gives an excellent definition for anxiety and helps outline what it seeks to accomplish in the lives of its victims. This dictionary defines anxiety as "an abnormal and overwhelming sense of apprehension and fear often marked by physiological signs (as sweating, tension, and increased pulse), by doubt concerning the reality and nature of the threat, and by self-doubt about one's capacity to cope with it."[7]

Anxiety for millions of people creates a troubling of the mind for an uncertain event, but it is even more than that. An etymology of this word provides some fascinating insight, because *anxious* comes from the Latin word *anxius* which means "to choke, to cause distress". A related word means "tightness or narrowness[8]." Anxiety is a word that expresses the painful impressions, physiological reactions, and mental uneasiness that comes over you. Most people who struggle with this express that they do not even really know where the anxiousness is coming from or what is happening within them, but the effects are nonetheless taking effect. Although there may be thoughts accompanying anxiety, many times one does not even know the clear object of the anxiousness, especially when it comes to what is professionally called Generalized Anxiety Disorder (GAD). It is a presence that seems to loom and swell without relenting.

Stress

You probably will not complete a full day without hearing the word *stress* used to express the toll that life takes on many people you interact with on a daily basis. Stress speaks of a pressure that comes on us during adversarial circumstances and intense situations that become punishing. This pressing down can come from perceived external sources or from within. Interestingly enough, part of Merriam-Webster's first definition for stress is "a physical, chemical, or emotional factor that causes bodily or mental tension and may be a factor in disease causation." Today stress is being considered more and more as a major root cause for many mental ailments and even physical diseases that plague humanity. If ignored or overlooked, stress can have major long term effects on people, especially through mind and body connections. But what you will see later in this writing is that stress is simply just another word to describe layers of fear that are seeking to bring torment and keep you from your peace.

Panic

Panic speaks of what we know as "panic attacks", which has become a very familiar term today. This word has gained additional use socially, yet it has also become a medically diagnosable issue. Panic is a predominant issue with people suffering from anxiety disorders. The background of the word panic is based in the Greek language and in mythology. Panic comes from the word "pan" which is what the Greeks named one of the demon gods.[9] It is a word used to describe terror and immobility that comes with certain triggers. It creates emotional paralysis, sweating, dizziness, hot flashes, chills, and can lead to deep feelings of loneliness.

Phobia

We get our current word "fear" from the word phobia, but today we use this word to describe a specific fear that creates a "fight or flight" response. The word phobia originally meant "flight," which gives the expression of what fear does. It pushes you to run away from and avoid the trigger or source that appears to be fearful. Thousands of phobias exist. In fact, there are resources online that take pride in listing the massive number of phobias that exist. If you can name something, most likely there is a phobia of it documented.

Timidity

This word means "to fear, or to be easily frightened." It also means "to be shy," describing a feeling of fear under the pressure of another person or situation because of a lack of boldness and courage. Timidity kicks in when one is under the pressure of another person or force.

Fear

The definition of fear is defined as "an uneasiness of a person upon the thought of future evil likely to fall on them.[10]" It looks towards the future and projects images and thoughts of evil and destruction taking place in some form or fashion.

All these words have become a greater part of our culture in many ways. In the next few chapters, we will further identify fear related disorders as well as the tactics that fear uses and we shall see how it affects our lives.

---

[1] http://www.merriam-webster.com/dictionary/terrorism
[2] http://www.washingtonpost.com/wp-dyn/articles/A40571-2004Mar31.html
[3] My intent is *not* to tell people that all movies, video games, and roller coaster rides are wrong or evil. Please don't interpret that. What I am attempting to bring out is the truth that fear surrounds us and has subtle ways of getting into our lives, our way of thinking, and our beliefs more than we sometimes realize.
[4] http://people.howstuffworks.com/halloween6.htm
[5] Proverbs 29:25
[6] http://www.m-w.com/dictionary/worry

[7] http://www.m-w.com/dictionary/anxiety
[8] http://www.etymonline.com/index.php?term=anxious
[9] http://www.etymonline.com/index.php?term=panic
[10] This is the tormenting definition of fear and is not to be confused with *the fear of the Lord*, which is a healthy awe and respect for His person and presence.

Chapter 2

Fear FACT-ors

So what is fear doing to our society and culture? The facts are astounding, and more is being discovered. The National Institute of Mental Health believes that an estimated 26.2 percent of Americans 18 or older (more then one quarter of the adult population) suffers from a diagnosable mental disorder. This figure targets approximately 57.7 million people in the United States alone. Additionally, mental disorders have become the leading cause of disability in the U.S. and Canada for ages 15-44.[1] Anxiety disorders affect at least 40 million Americans above the age of 18,[2] and anxiety disorders are the number one mental health problem with women. It is the number two disorder with men, second only to drug abuse and alcoholism[3]. This does not even cover the millions of people who may be suffering silently and have not received any help, and those who are battling with low levels of fear, but won't deal with them until the effects become debilitating. In addition, research is even confirming that stress, worry and anxiety can be root causes for many diseases that people are battling.

Statistically, women suffer from anxiety and stress almost twice as much as men. Anxiety disorders are among the most common mental illnesses in America. It is beginning to surpass a related mental disorder, depression, in numbers. Anxiety is the most common health issue of Americans 65 and older and it is costing our country 47 billion dollars annually.

There are many mental ailments that are rooted in fear. Many of these can be researched extensively online or through well organized references such at The Merck Manual[4] or Mayo Clinic Family Health Book.[5] As you research, you will find certain categories to these disorders. The following are some main groupings that are included in this category:

Panic Attacks and Panic Disorders

A panic attack is a sudden onset of at least four symptoms which include chest pain, discomfort, choking, dizziness, faintness, feelings of insanity, hot flashes, detachment from reality, flushes, chills, numbness, tingling sensations, accelerated heart rate, shortness of breath, sweating, shaking, and others. Many times these symptoms subside in a few minutes, but when they become chronic, it is considered a disorder. Panic issues typically begin in late adolescence or during early childhood. These attacks often come unexpectedly and many who struggle with this disorder also have a fear of the panic attacks returning again in the future.

Phobias

This type of anxiety disorder is one that is fixed on an external stimulus. In today's society, we now have names for almost every kind of specific fear, including some that you would never think existed. Web sites can even be found online that have attempted to document each one and put them in alphabetical listings.[6] Interestingly enough, the majority of fears do not make sense to the average observer.

Jerry Seinfeld, a well known comedian, has made note of the fact that the number one fear in America is public speaking. The number two fear is death. He jokes that the average American would rather be lying in the casket than giving the eulogy in front of people. Who said fear made sense!

On a more serious note, Time magazine published an article on the topic of fear and phobias in our society, which helped shed some light on the serious effect it is having.

> *The list of identified phobias is expanding every day and is now, of course, collected online . . . where more than 500 increasingly quirky human fears are labeled, sometimes tongue-in-cheek, and cataloged alphabetically. Some have more to do with neology than psychology. (It's one thing to invent a word like arachibutyrophobia, another thing to find someone who's really afraid of peanut butter sticking to the roof of the mouth.) Other phobias, however--like acrophobia (fear of heights), claustrophobia (fear of enclosed spaces) and agoraphobia (a crushing, paralyzing terror of anything outside the safety of the home)--can be deadly*

serious business. If the names of phobias can be found online, the people who actually suffer from at least one of them at some point in their life--about 50 million in the U.S. by some estimates--are everywhere. They may be like "Beth," a pseudonym, a middle school student in Boston whose hemophobia, or fear of blood, was so severe that even a figure of speech like "cut it out" could make her faint. Or they may be like "Jean," 38, an executive assistant in New Jersey who is so terrified of balloons that just walking into a birthday party can make her break out in a sweat.[7]

Obsessive Compulsive Disorders

This category of disorder is well known by its initials and the way it is culturally expressed. Although many times spoken in jest, people express certain personal quirks by saying they are having an "OCD fit" or an "OCD attack." Obsessive Compulsive Disorders bring tremendous torment to an individual, especially in the area of repetitive mental attacks. These attacks drive and induce the person toward "mental spirals" and very addictive behaviors. Medical resources express these compulsions as "repetitive behaviors (e.g., hand washing, ordering, checking) or mental acts (e.g., praying, counting, repeating words silently) that the person feels driven to perform in response to an obsession, or according to rules that must be applied rigidly. The behaviors or mental acts are aimed at preventing or reducing distress or preventing some dreaded event or situation; however, these behaviors or mental acts either are not connected in a realistic way with what they are designed to neutralize or prevent or are clearly excessive."[8] Although linked to other root issues, fear is a major factor in this disorder.

Post Traumatic Stress Disorders

Post Traumatic Stress (PTS) Disorders are connected to a very significant trauma that has taken place in a person's life. The event is experienced continually in the person's memory and is reinforced with intense fear, dread and/or terror in relation to that event. Avoidance of that event or any future interaction with a related event becomes a significant coping mechanism. This can be well illustrated by soldiers who have fought through intense battles overseas and come home still replaying the traumas and live in torment over them. It can happen to someone who ends up in a tragic accident or any kind of intense event that creates mental or physical trauma.

Depression

Although depression is not always linked with fear and anxiety issues, there are some similarities in these two disorders. Both anxiety and depression are the result of low serotonin levels and both disorders deal with a loss of reality, hope and perspective. In my experience helping people, many times someone who deals with an anxiety disorder for a long period of time can lose hope and slip into depression. I have also found that many of the same methods for getting victory over anxiety can help defeat depression and other mental conditions as well.

Depression is definitely an ailment that affects the entire person in that there are physical, spiritual, and psychological effects from it. Someone suffering with severe depression cannot merely "get over it" because he or she has been consumed with some level of hopelessness. It affects the way they eat, sleep, and live their lives. Motivation becomes harder to draw from as self-esteem and self-image have become tampered with. A growing number of people are also suffering from bipolar, a relative of depression and is a mood condition marked with extreme manic highs and lows in a person's emotional stability and behavior. Although this book is not focusing on a lot of the specifics regarding depression and bipolar, much of the principles found in these pages are transferable in gaining victory over them.

Fear Connections

The fascinating truth is that medical research is showing in increasing evidence, the strong connection of anxiety and stress to disease, especially when it comes to the immune system. Running in top condition, our immune system are designed to run at such an efficient capacity that health and balance is maintained in the body. Yet one of the greatest physical vulnerabilities is when this system is not working in proper order. As we will see in later chapters, fear, stress, and anxiety can be the biggest enemies that come against the inner workings of the immune system.

For centuries, people knew that disease factors greatly increase when fear, stress, and anxiety were at work in the lives of people. But as society became more sophisticated and advanced, this belief was put on the back shelf. Yet in the past few decades, more research groups, including the medical community are acknowledging the major connection between stress and disease.[9] In fact, it is becoming increasingly evident that behind many emotional disorders and physical diseases lies a root of fear that has compromised health and vitality. We will unlock this more in the pages ahead.

---

[1] http://www.nimh.nih.gov/healthinformation/statisticsmenu.cfm

[2] http://www.nimh.nih.gov/publicat/anxiety.cfm

[3] http://www.conqueranxiety.com/anxiety_statistics.asp

[4] The Merck Manual used to research for this writing was the following: Merck & Co.. *The Merck Manual: Seventeenth Edition.* West Point, PA: Merck & Co., Inc., 2004.

[5] Mayo Clinic. *Mayo Clinic Family Health Book.* New York, NY: Collins, 3rd edition (May 6, 2003)

[6] http://www.phobialist.com

[7] http://www.time.com/time/printout/0,8816,999584,00.html

[8] http://psychcentral.com/disorders/sx25.htm

[9] http://www.mindtools.com/stress/UnderstandStress/StressHealth.htm
http://www.nih.gov/news/WordonHealth/oct2000/story01.htm

Chapter 3

God's Marvelous Design

The amazing fact is that God designed our body to be able to handle the temporary fears and stresses of this life in a dynamic way. The human anatomy as intended by our Creator was fashioned to have a very complex, yet intricately effective system to handle the adversarial situations that we face. This system is known in many circles as the "Fight or Flight response." [1]

The Hypothalamus

In your brain there is a tiny, yet extremely significant organ called the hypothalamus, which plays an important role in both your endocrine and limbic systems. As a part of the endocrine system, the hypothalamus is responsible for secreting hormones throughout the bloodstream to organs in order to control metabolism, growth, development, and reproduction. [2] But as a member of the limbic system, this same gland contributes to the regulation of blood pressure, heart rate, hunger, thirst, sexual arousal and function, and sleeping patterns. [3] The hypothalamus also links the body's endocrine system to the nervous system by way of the pituitary gland, which is instrumental in creating a general sense of calmness and stability in the body—a state called *homoeostasis*.

The hypothalamus is a critical member because it acts as a thermostat or control center for what takes place in your body. It also contributes, along with other glands in the body, to the control of a process known as the "fight or flight response." As a simple example, if a bear was to suddenly jump out at you from the woods and attack you, your body would instantly enter into this entire process immediately and automatically. Fight or flight is an involuntary system that does not need your direction or attention. The crisis presents itself, and your body automatically reacts. You don't have to tell your body, "there's a bear coming so its time to panic and react." Your body is already pre-programmed and designed to automatically kick in the mechanisms necessary.

If I came up to you from behind and screamed, you would most likely become startled. The more unexpected the scream, the more you would probably react. Your body would automatically kick in and enter into a momentary state of minor shock. Then your body would execute other processes to help bring you back to calmness again. As soon as you realize that it was just me attempting to surprise you, your brain knows there's nothing to be afraid of and it can bring the body back to homeostasis.

Humans can achieve extraordinary victories in crisis because of the process that the "fight or fight response" brings to the situation. This explains why a parent has been able to pick up the back end of a car to save their child who is trapped under it. Human strength and resourcefulness compound rapidly to astonishing levels during stressful situations as energy and focus rises to the occasion.

The hypothalamus receives a signal that you are in a fearful situation and begins to initiate a complex process throughout your body before you can even consciously think about it. Signals are being sent to create action. All kinds of mechanisms are occurring during this progression without your permission, and most likely without your knowledge.

Cortisol

There is also a chemical that is released in your body that's worth mentioning called cortisol. This hormone gets secreted throughout your body during "fight or flight" through your adrenal glands and has a major role in helping to supply the energy needed to face the intense situation at hand. Cortisol is sent into the blood stream to help give you the energy needed to escape or survive a crisis situation. It also aids in bringing greater focus to your mind and it lowers your vulnerability to pain for that temporary situation. Yet one thing is very clear, increased levels of cortisol will result in pulling resources from certain body systems in order for the person to have the necessary energy to survive.

Let's go back to the example of a bear jumping out at you in the woods. In this "fight or flight" moment, cortisol is secreted and begins to spread to multiple areas of your body. It travels to your reproductive system and acquires resources from it. There is certainly no need for sexual activity in this situation because the highest priority is running from a bear. Cortisol also takes energy from your digestive system and begins to shut down parts of it so that more energy can be used for the crisis. It is not time to eat; it is time to run from the bear, wouldn't you agree? Do you ever notice that when you are in fearful or anxious situations, there can be a loss of appetite? [4]

It is imperative to know that there is another system that gets depleted of resources when "fight/flight" is in action and that is the immune system. Because you are encountering a moment of crisis, you obviously do not need to fight off a cold or a disease right now. Your body's primary focus is to run from the bear, an undertaking which will require as much energy and resource as possible. Yet when the immune system becomes tapped out for too long, major problems begin to set in.

When a person remains in a chronic state or pattern of stress and anxiety, the immune system loses its ability to efficiently and effectively fight off invaders of sickness in the body. That is why medical professionals will consider fear, stress, and anxiety as potential contributors to many diseases and ailments that people have. Although many professionals do not consider the stress factor highly enough, many doctors will often ask patients about their personal stress levels and explore areas where there is extensive strain on their emotional well being. In many cases, the cause behind what is happening physically has a link to what is taking place in an unseen realm of thought that has created multiple "stressors."

Personal Experience

In my own personal journey, I was plagued with a number of sicknesses and ailments that just seemed to continue in an endless cycle. I became very frustrated, especially since I was in an active pastoral role in a large church. I needed to be well and healthy so I could have enough energy throughout the day, but I found I was continually hitting a brick wall. Among my pastoral responsibilities, I also led worship for our multiple services, which required stamina and endurance. In addition to that, I also oversaw our mass church productions that we presented regularly.

During this time of church ministry, I was having physical struggles and infirmities. Along with the torment that anxiety and depression brought to me, I also had to deal with many other physical ailments: seasonal allergies, chronic sinus infections, cat allergies, stomach issues including hiatal hernias and acid reflux (which sent me to the hospital a few times in incredible pain) and insomnia. In addition, I was constantly getting sick and to make matters worse, I was also losing a sense of emotional stability.

After hearing my story, many would say that I probably just needed a vacation or I should have considered taking more breaks. The problem is that I certainly did that. I tried everything I could to get relief, including prescription drugs, but the problems were never fully removed until I personally dealt with the fear issues in my life that had forced my immune system to malfunction. One by one, when the areas of fear were confronted and mended, I noticed in a matter of days that my immune system began working at a higher capacity, because I started to get well. I no longer needed the prescription meds I had for my stomach problems and for the generalized anxiety I suffered with.

To this day, I no longer have consistent allergies, including cat allergies that used to send me into a sneezing tailspin. I also do not struggle with acid reflux problems or the hiatal hernias. I sleep much better and longer. When I got rid of the workings of fear in my life, homeostasis was possible as my hypothalamus and other organs began to regulate my body levels. When fear is confronted head on and removed, there are massive changes that take place in sanity and in health. It is God's original design for living.

Cortisol Effects and Chronic Fear

Increased cortisol levels also halt the operation of important interleukins and macrophages that serve the body in powerful ways. Macrophages attack pathogens and infectious agents to preserve health in your body. There are also multiple interleukins in your system that contribute to immunity and health in the body by performing a litany of tasks, from creating a fever which will fight off a sickness, to attacking cancer cells and destroying them. Yet when cortisol levels are heightened, these agents cannot fight off those invaders, which leave your body susceptible to sickness and disease.

So this leads us to the predicament that is vital to recognize and cannot be overlooked. When a person has a pattern of chronic fear, stress or anxiety at any level of intensity, this process of "fight or flight" is occurring in endless loops. In addition to this endless cycle is the buffeting that the body's reproductive system, digestive system, and immune system are taking. When this occurs, the person enters into a persistent sequence that medical professionals call the "General Adaptation Syndrome" (GAS). This process takes place in three stages, the alarm stage, the adaptation/resistance stage and the exhaustion stage.

The Alarm Stage

The alarm stage initiates the process when a fearful situation or thought presents itself and the body reacts. Messages are sent throughout your body, telling you, "Let's go! Run! Move! You're in trouble! Better get out of here! You're not safe!" or "Do something quick and defend yourself!" Tension begins to develop in your chest and tightness manifests itself in your throat. Shortness of breath and perspiration are common as well. Meanwhile your muscles begin to throb with vigor as adrenaline gets pumped into your system, giving you seemingly "superman" strength. Your pupils begin to dilate as your mind develops an intense focus on the situation at hand. This is all part of the system that God intricately designed so that you could run from a dangerous circumstance. In a normal circumstance, certain parts of the nervous system (the parasympathetic nervous system) initiates a course of action that brings you back to calmness and homeostasis.

Yet when GAS is in a chronic repetitive operation, the nervous system does not have a chance to bring the body back to peace. The fear response is still being executed repeatedly. For someone struggling with fear issues, it is not an issue of a bear running at them. It could be their boss. It could be their future, their spouse, the situation their child is in, finances, security, a mother-in-law or any number of things. Furthermore, as I discussed earlier regarding anxiety, there may not be a clear object of fear at all. Fear may be projecting something that is totally in their thoughts and nowhere to be found in physical reality. When this process continues its loop, we are led into the second phase of GAS.

Adaptation / Resistance Stage

If the cause for stress, anxiety and worry is not resolved, your body makes an attempt to get accustomed to this "fight or flight" state for long term protection. It is at this point that the body has realized that the alarm stage is not temporary, but will remain in process for an indefinite amount of time. Although you were not designed for long-term adaptation of stress, your organs and faculties do their best to maintain survival. Unfortunately, our culture is so driven and intense that millions live in this state for very long spans of time. For some it is even a regular way of living. Our bodies can get away with this resistance stage for a certain amount of time, but after a while it becomes increasingly threatening to our good health. At this stage, the "fight or flight" responses are firing in repeated fashion without much of a break or relief. The body in fact increases it resource withdrawal from the different organ systems as cortisol is continually secreted.

Exhaustion Stage

At the exhaustion stage, the effects of anxiety and stress on a person are beginning to show signs of wear and tear. It is at this junction that the body really starts to wear out and reveals the fact that we were not designed to be in this state for too long at all. The adrenal glands at this point have been constantly pumping adrenaline to the extent that the body ends up living on fumes, while progressively moving towards exhaustion. The body also has been worked up, focused, and drilled on this specific fear or multiple fears and now there is no avoiding the exhaustion.

The sad reality is that we have folks in and out of the church that are struggling with this issue. Fear is no respecter of persons. The church today is being attacked by fear and is burnt out. What makes matters worse is that too many have adapted to fear-driven living to the point that it gets defended. They end up saying things like, "I'm not really in stress. This isn't a fear issue. I just have a lot of work and responsibilities." The habit gets defended and the cycle continues.

For someone dealing with stress and anxiety in chronic form; when the exhaustion hits, depression finds an open door to enter in. The reason depression can enter is because hope is harder to see during times of fear, especially when the person has been deeply programmed to be driven to work, go, clean, do, think, and talk to the point of exhaustion. Once exhaustion sets in, the issues of life that have been masked and ignored for years are now exposed and are causing an oppression of despair and depression. Meaninglessness, hopelessness and heaviness have a vulnerable place to attack as this person is now lost in a state of burnout.

Sadly, this is happening all over our country and across the world. It has become pandemic in the United States and one of the reasons is because we are such a driven nation. We move and go and we cannot seem to stop. The next appointment is coming. The meeting is right around the corner. The next event needs to be prepared for. Whenever free time is made available, there is an incessant drive to fill it with more tasks and more chores to complete.

Understand this: God never designed us as His creation to live this way. He did not create us for hyper speed travel and light speed, microwavable results in race car timing. In all truthfulness, *He really designed us for camel travel*. Instead of only focusing on the destination, our bodies were intended to experience the peace and joy that comes when we simply enjoy the ride that leads us to the destination. Yet, today people seem to just want to get to the bottom line and to the end target as quickly as possible, so that another task can be stuffed into the schedule. Yet according to camel travel, it takes some time and patience to set out on a particular passage. According to camel travel, if you were going to take a trip to New York from Chicago, you would have to get the camel ready, pack your bags and get prepared for a lengthy trip. Yet along the way you would experience many adventures that would add value to your life, all while teaching you the joy of a patient journey experienced.

Instead we find ourselves today in a totally different environment, filled with fast-paced deadlines that seem to progressively get more jam-packed. The heartbreaking result is that millions of people are struggling with fear-based disorders and diseases and don't know how to get well, because popular culture is being driven by the same fear. The result is that many are left without answers. They're consumed with so many struggles and conflicts and no one has taught them what to do with the fearful thoughts and pressures. Meanwhile, God is calling out with a much better way to live.

Making the Connection

Articles and reports have been coming out in greater numbers, illuminating the connection between fear, stress and anxiety and many of the diseases and ailments that the world battles. One recent article I ran into was found in a section called, "Health Smart", written by Dr. Tedd Mitchell for USA Weekend on March 2-4, 2007. In this particular article, Dr. Mitchell conveys the blessings of adrenaline, yet also shows how "fight or flight" has been working against our bodies. He also confirms that even if this process occurs continually in small doses, the consequences can still become very harmful.

When placed under extreme stress, the body prepares itself to face danger through the release of hormones from the adrenal glands (hence, the term adrenaline). Increased heart rate, dilation of the lungs' airways for deeper breathing, redirection of blood flow from the digestive organs to the large muscle groups of the body -- these changes occur immediately when the human body is placed under extreme duress. It's a wonderful system that gives us the capacity to do extraordinary things under extraordinarily stressful circumstances. It is rapid, intense and short-lived, and it comes in real handy when the house is on fire. Unfortunately, that same system is activated, to a lesser degree, when we face the day-to-day dramas of life. This is when the system really begins to work against us.

The problem with stress reactions is that they sneak up on you. The tensions of daily life don't sound alarms in the body like a house fire does. Symptoms of chronic stress often masquerade as other things: headaches, insomnia, heartburn, chest pain, sexual issues -- the list goes on and on. These symptoms need to be addressed appropriately because many medical problems have stress as a common denominator. And if stress isn't even on our radar screen as a possible contributor to our problems, then we'll never get the help we need.[5]

The Truth Will Make You Free

The certainty that you can come to by the end of this book and through understanding God's Word is that no matter the name; anxiety, stress, panic, horror or terror, the trail leads back to the same root word: fear. Throughout the pages of this book, we will break down the work of fear and defeat it. This revelation will also have strong application with it so that immense freedom and healing can come forth. In these days, God is going to give the church an inside look into what is tormenting people. In addition, we will see what is behind the diseases and ailments that have brought anguish to people who need an opportunity to be liberated.

Through breaking the bondage of fear, the church is going to see people set free from anxiety, stress and worry in greater numbers. The body of Christ is also going to regain a new level of discernment that will reveal the strategies that fear uses. As we understand the spirit, mind and body connections associated with fear, we will witness a greater dimension of physical healings. As we learn to break the power of fear, our immune systems will begin to operate in the way God originally designed. Not only will anxiety and mental illnesses be cured, but diseases and disorders such as MCS/EI, allergies, auto-immune diseases, ulcers, irritable bowel syndromes, insomnia, thyroid dysfunctions, high blood pressure, lowered immunity, weight issues, heart disease, sexual dysfunctions and many more will be healed as the power of fear is broken in their lives.[6]

Not only does God want to heal you, but His desire is for you to be in health and live your life without the oppression of fear. This is powerfully expressed in one of John's letters to the church that shared his heart's prayer for them.

Beloved, I pray that you may prosper in all things and be in health, just as your soul prospers.
3 John 1:2 (NKJV)

My prayer for you is that God will reveal himself in power to heal and deliver you from the power of fear and bring you into divine health and prosperous living. It is time for you to understand your enemy and wage war to regain the health that has been lost. Are you ready to keep on reading?

---

[1] For the overall purposes I have in this book, I did not spend an extensive amount of time on the physiology section, but it can be a valuable pathway of research, especially in understanding the effect of fear, stress, and anxiety on the human body. I would encourage you to further study on some basic human anatomy concepts to help you in understanding how God created your body to operate. Don't let it overwhelm you because in today's age there is a multitude of web sites and reference guides that simplify the terms. Some topics to research are: "Fight/Flight Response", "Endocrine System", "Limbic System", "hypothalamus", and "nervous system" – including sympathetic and parasympathetic nervous systems.

[2] http://en.wikipedia.org/wiki/Endocrine_system

[3] http://en.wikipedia.org/wiki/Limbic_system

[4] Anxiety, stress and worry can have varying effects on digestive systems and appetites. Some can end up having all kinds of digestive problems from ulcers to irritable bowel syndrome. Fear issues can cause some to *lose* their appetite, while others will eat obsessively to calm their fears in an attempt to bring a temporary sense of peace and nurturing.

[5] http://www.usaweekend.com/07_issues/070304/070304healthsmart.html

[6] Fear is not the only underlying root behind many diseases (there are many other areas that could be covered), but for the purpose of this book, we will focus on *fear* and its effects.

Chapter 4

Is Fear Working in You?

So the honest question we have to ask ourselves is, "Do I have fear working in my life?" The greater our personal sincerity in response to this query, the faster we will enter the path to freedom. When we honestly ask God to speak to our hearts and reveal if fear is trying to work its way into our thought processes, beliefs, identity, relationships, and way of life, we begin a journey towards freedom on a solid step. For many, the true answer to that question may be a surprise. At the same time, we have to remember that there is no need to go into major guilt and introspection on this matter. The reality is that in today's society, the odds are extremely high of the answer being, "Yes, fear is operating in my life."

Yet when confronted with this inquiry, many will react with defensiveness, covering their actions and motives with various statements of avoidance:

"No, I don't really have fear. I'm just very concerned."
"This is a *good* fear that I have. It's a *healthy* fear."
"We'll I'm basically a nervous and anxious person."
"There's not much I can do about it. I'm simply stressed out."

These are all phrases frequently spoken, yet they usually reflect some type of fear working within. When we honestly examine the motivations behind the words that come out of our mouth, we will realize the trap that we continually fall into. Others may say something like, "I can't help myself. I'm just a worried person."

In these last two statements fear is not only at work, but the person has also made it a part of their identity. "I *am* a worried person. I *am* an anxious person." This statement implies, "this is who I am. This is me and it's what I'm most likely going to continue to be."

In order to have victory over fear, there will need to be an illumination in our hearts that fear has been the source of many of our thoughts and actions. Of course it is essential that we receive this in love, and not condemnation.

The Fear of the Lord

On the flip side, there is a "fear of the Lord" that the Scriptures speak of, but it is a completely different fear that produces different results. The fear that does not come from God produces torment. The fear of the Lord produces a reverential awe and respect for the glory of God. This healthy awe will enhance divine hunger within us to know God more and draw near to His presence. The fear of the Lord is not intended to send us running away in terror and avoidance. In fact, it will stir up a seeking heart of worship that not only receives His love, but yearns for a deeper touch of His presence. The fear of the Lord keeps us humble, leads us to repentance and reminds us of the splendor and wonder of God's majesty. This biblical fear is not the kind of fear that I am talking about. The fear I am speaking of in this book is a *spirit of fear*.

Unveiling Fear's Game

Fear is working behind the scenes in numerous ways, yet too many people are blind to its activity and to the realization of how many strings it is pulling. Scores of well meaning people spend their existence being sucked into fear ridden lifestyles. They end up justifying and rationalizing their fear-based actions, yet humble heart-felt recognition is our first step towards overcoming.

Here is just a simple list of many common fears that our enemy tries to put into our lives. This is by no means an exhaustive list. But I'm sure you can relate to at least a few.

Fear of Evil • Fear of the Future • Fear of Failure • Fear of Rejection • Fear of Abandonment • Fear of Man/Intimidation • Dread/Terror/Horror • Phobias - there are thousands • Fear of Death/Disease • Anxiety• Worry • Fear of Not Being Delivered • Being Scared of God • Fear of Not Being Safe • Night Terrors • Fear of Confrontation • Perfectionism • Drivenness • Control • Fear of Authority Figures • Fear of Being Hurt •Manipulation

---

Fear Focus and Trauma

As you will discover in the pages ahead, fear has a way of placing a narrow focal point on a certain issue, event, person, or object while emphasizing the torment and insecurity relating to it. Whenever the specific fear makes an appearance, the person under its influence will usually have a strong reaction of avoidance and panic. Unless recognized and confronted, this specific fear will work overtime to magnify its impact on the individual, and to direct the individual's focus and attention on it. Also, in many cases the fears have roots leading back to childhood experiences or to traumas that have reinforced the fear.

Traumas are open-door events where fear can storm in and reinforce the fright of that painful event. At this doorpoint, fear can enter and partner with the traumatic event and use it as a trigger to support its future assaults. Fear projects that trauma on the screen of the mind, with an emphasis on fearfully avoiding that pain in the future at all costs. The ultimate goal becomes to never experience that dreadful event ever again. A trauma can be anything that shocks your system: a car accident, a verbally, physically or sexually abusive situation, an injury or a moment of rejection.

For example, a person who has been severely abused will usually be left extremely vulnerable. Fear will seek to reinforce that event of victimization, emphasizing a fear of rejection and uncleanness that can leave the person unable to give and receive love freely. Because of this, often they are unable to fully release themselves into intimacy with future relationships. The projection of their past pain casts a shadow of dread, keeping them from truly breaking out into new experiences. The fear of the past repeating itself again is way too frightening. The power of those traumas needs to be broken and the doorways that it created need to be closed in order to make way for freedom and liberty.

Doorpoints for Fear

Fear will always look for any doorpoint to enter in and bring torment to us. This usually occurs when we are the most vulnerable and broken. Fear can enter in our teenage years, adulthood or surprisingly, even at birth. Different markers along our journey can generate fearful imprints in our lives that create tremendous difficulties in living freely and being able to take risks.

Let me illustrate this point. Those who struggle with a fear of poverty or a fear of "not having enough" can come under that influence; allowing it to be a driving motivation to work as hard as they possibly can, many times to unhealthy degrees. Although diligence is a valuable trait, many times this intense driven work ethic is motivated by the fear of going broke or not being able to pay the bills. Many times you will hear very wealthy people in the business world admit that what motivates them to work hard and long is a fear of ever going back to poverty. In these cases, you can usually trace their lives back to some point where they did not feel financially stable or have a sense of security when it came to work and making money. So fear steps in and compels the person to do whatever it takes not to let poverty happen. Survival mode sets in.

Many times, those who seem to have the hardest time realizing that fear is driving their life are those who have achieved tremendous success because of their fears. They drove themselves on a daily basis to no end, working for that last dollar to avoid poverty at all costs. They are admired by many, yet deep down inside they are riddled with a fear that will never let them be at peace and content financially. They are driven to keep the monster of fear fed. For a multitude of others, the fear of poverty becomes a self-fulfilling prophecy because they believed what fear told them. They entertained thoughts of poverty each day and now they are living that curse; a bad dream that has become reality. Now they are financially stuck and do not know how to get out. Escaping this situation would involve risk, yet risk is not a part this person's mindset because that would involve *facing fear*. It is important to remember that is very difficult to stand up to fear and take a risk when you are indeed *serving* fear.

Fear Fulfilled

One of the big reasons why fear has had such power over people is because of the nature of its message. Fear will cause one of two reactionary pathways in those who give in to its calling. One of those reactions is *avoidance* or *displacement*. A person under the influence of a specific fear will do anything and everything to stay away from that fearful situation or will remove himself if found caught in that very scenario. For the most part, a person who fears rejection will stay away from public speaking. Those who fear being in crowds will stay at home. Those who fear the future will never do anything risky. Those who have a phobia will never be seen close to their phobic stimulus.

The other reaction that fear brings is the self-fulfilled prophecy of doom. In this case, *that which you fear comes upon you*. Because fear brings such a narrow focus on an issue, one becomes obsessed with it and eventually lives out the very thing once feared. When this ensues, the problem escalates because fear has now become reality, thus leaving a sturdier foundation for the next fear to stand on. This proves that really all we have to fear is fear itself, if we let ourselves do so. For example, many who fear rejection end up feeling rejected anyway. Those who fear the future end up having some tough breaks, especially because they spent so much time obsessing about what could go wrong, rather than what could go right. Meanwhile they were missing out on the great things of life, never realizing that the majority of what they fear, never even happens.

We Have Been Deceived by Fear

The more we honestly search our hearts and lives on this subject of fear, we begin to see how we have been deeply programmed to think and act out of fear, rather than out of power, love, and a sound mind. Today fear's tactics are becoming more and more covert. Often in our church circles, fear begins a masquerade by cloaking itself in the disguise of *concern* and *good judgment*. We pat ourselves on the back for making great decisions that we give credit to the Lord for, yet the choices were motivated by what fear was projecting. The fear of man has become such a powerful snare that people in the body of Christ *live* to avoid being rejected or labeled negatively so they never have a solid chance to operate by faith. What drives too many congregations is an intimidation that has concealed itself behind a mask of man's wisdom. Our political games and Judas kissing practices are praised as manifold wisdom when in reality we are neck deep in the clutches of the fear of man. The problem is, no one wants to stand up boldly against this dysfunction because it has now become such a strong cultural way of living.

As you can see, fear will find any avenue or side street to drive through. It can start with simple worry that builds into a massive daily fear of the future. A trauma of abandonment as a young child can give room for fear to bring pressure and stress regarding emotional safety and security. Night terrors during childhood can allow room for fear to come in and program a person to never feel safe when going to bed. Performance-driven homes pressure young people to perform and excel at all costs all the way into adulthood. In too many areas, fear is *driving* us instead of our most holy faith in God *leading* us. There is a huge difference that we are going to begin to see.

Yet most of all, what fear has done for so many, is that it has broken the hearts of millions and has kept them from their eternal destiny. During this process, I am praying that God would begin to show you the path to freedom and give you a touch from His hand that heals your heart on a daily basis. As we continue, I invite you to pause and give God an "all access pass" to your heart so that He can bring illumination and truth.

I invite you to continue with me as we discover together the truth about fear by finding out what the Scriptures say about it. Then later on, we will see how we can break free from it.

Section II

What the Scriptures Say About Fear

Chapter 5

Fear Has Torment

"fear hath torment . . ."
1 John 4:18

Torment is the very nature and essence of fear. In the Scriptures, the word translated "torment" describes a continual process of inflicted punishment in a person's life. The materialization of this torment does not necessarily always imply physical beatings or Chinese water torture. Yet fear's manifestation can have severely afflicting effects emotionally. Sometimes physical pain can bow in comparison to the mental anguish that fear brings. Fear will act as a terrorist and cause its victim to narrowly focus on the torment at hand and will continue to do so indefinitely. The more this happens, the more fear appears as the master reality with greater intensity. Thoughts come crashing to the mind, saying things such as,

"I need to get that one thing solved."
"How am I going to be able to make it?"
"I better do well on this or I am sunk."
"What if I never find a job?"
"I just need to take care of these issues, and then I can settle down."
"What if I never marry?"
"If this would just leave me alone I would be ok."
"What if this anxiety never ends?"
"I am going to end up poor and alone."

Thoughts begin to swirl around, creating all kinds of mental instability. Questions begin to arise as to the nature and reason for this constant thought process and focus. Logical answers do not seem to solve the stress, so obsession begins to take shape, sometimes leading to sheer panic. With that obsession, a person begins to lose out on receiving the wonderful things of the day, because he cannot get his mind off of this "thing."

Torment's Secret Weapon: What If?

"What about this?" and "What if" are the favorite phrases of fear. Each time such words invade the mind, there is a specific intent to bring a mental projection of doom, gloom and failure. "What if I get a disease?" or "What about your low bank account?" and "What if you can't pay your bills this month?" are examples of this kind of talk. Even when a person attempts to be at peace, fear will slide in with its torment to remind them that things are not as well as they hoped.

Any room of insecurity is used as a window to incite questions of doubt and uncertainty, thus making a positive outlook nearly impossible. The "what if's" all point to a scenario that can *seem* realistic to the individual. Yet as folks begin to get victory over fear, they will recognize that the weapons of fear are all simply a spectacle of fireworks, smoke and illusions. There is nothing realistic about fear's torment. It is only realistic if we give it that validation. We are only the victims of that which we fear anyway. If fear is allowed in, it will have an increasing punishing effect as the slippery slope of growing anxious thoughts and worries do their job—torment.

The "What If" Solution

Jesus made it very clear when He said, "Therefore do not worry about tomorrow, for tomorrow will worry about its own things. Sufficient for the day *is* its own trouble."[1] Yet fear broadcasts its propaganda, driving us to worry and fret about the cares of this world. But Jesus promised us a divine peace as we release ourselves into the Father's care and simply focus on the work of today.

In addition we hear the instruction of the Apostle Peter saying, "Casting all your care upon Him, for He cares for you" (1 Peter 5:7). His love and care is the antidote to the torment that anxiety, worry and stress all try to bring into our lives. Notice how both Scriptural passages mentioned here deal with the everyday process of overcoming fear? Jesus commands us *each* day not to worry about tomorrow and Peter reminds us to continually cast the cares that daily rise up upon Him. The word *cast* in this passage does not speak of one action, but a continual practice of daily casting our cares upon God. Just as a fly fisherman repeatedly throws his line out into the water, we as God's children have the privilege of continually casting our concerns and worries into the refreshing waters of His love.

The Logic of Fear

Unfortunately for many, a vain attempt is made to reason with fear and use logic to chase it away. This may seem effective at first; however, ultimately this will fall short of producing solid long term results. Attempting to reason with fear or "debate it away" does not bring true resolution, because fear presents a vivid, yet false perspective. In fact, fear will find another angle from which to attack, rendering logic and analysis futile. For many, the mental games and anguish of the mind become exhausting when fear is on the scene.

Fear plants its seed in a breeding ground of insecurity, and increases that vulnerability by continually projecting doom into the future. Personally, I am reminded of times when I met with individuals who deeply wanted help for their struggles, yet their words glorified and emphasized the fear and torment that had enveloped their lives. They were so deeply programmed into fear's way of thinking that simple loving truth could not penetrate. "What if's" and "you better be careful" and "I hope that doesn't happen" were the main phrases used. They had been influenced by fear for so long that the thoughts of fear were reflected in the majority of the words they spoke. As this pattern repeatedly emerged, I began to realize that this issue was so complex that it needed to be dealt with on a supernatural level. We will get to that part very soon.

Fear also keeps us glued to the past traumas and mistakes that occurred in life, while at the same time projecting them into the future. It will also be quick to remind people of past failures and hurts with a strong message: *Do not get close to anything like that again.* Fear will seek to piggy back on moments of rejection or pain in our past and will attempt to program us into avoiding a repeat experience at all costs. New horizons of opportunities are viewed through lenses tinted with past failure, keeping people from stepping out into fresh experiences. Fear seeks to keep us bound to our past so that we cannot see a hopeful future.

Survival Method #1 – The Mask

Those who cannot get past the torment of fear seek to draw from survival devices intended to create protective barriers around their life. They believe that these devices are self-designed, yet in reality there is a work of the enemy who is seeking to prolong the prison sentence of fear-bondage. One such device is a fabricated personality. This mask offers a protective barrier, concealing the person's true identity, while projecting a false one. In short, this mask keeps people from seeing the "real you."

The lie spawned by fear is, "If they see who I really am and they do not like me, *I am all I have.* I've got nothing else to show them, so I will be sunk if they reject me. I do not want that to happen so I must protect myself." This lie becomes so hard wired that for many, the ability to "turn on" the mask becomes effortless and without conscious initiation.

I present these common masks for consideration: "the smart and intellectual person," "the composed and controlled person," or everyone's favorite, "the happy and funny person." In the church world, we find "the highly spiritual one" or the "mature Christian." We want people to have the impression that this is our true identity, yet the thing that is driving this deception is fear; and more specifically, a fear of rejection. Deep inside are severe wounds and fears, but the masks deceive us into believing that no one knows. Because so many are not secure in who they really are, putting on a fabricated personality seems to be more appealing.

As the pattern continues, people are conditioned to believe that this modality is actual working, and continue to use it. Meanwhile, destruction and dysfunction are brewing behind that facade. While the masquerade party is in session, the real identity suffers underneath. For those who use the fabricated personality to protect themselves from hurts and fears, the problems intensify and the pain increases. The damage continues to spread underneath because it is never brought to the surface. Torment now begins to fester beyond a level of conscious thinking.

Survival Method #2 – Drivenness

Millions, if not billions of people avoid dealing with fear issues by staying as busy as humanly possible. *Drivenness* has become a familiar practice in people who push themselves to work longer hours, accomplish more tasks, and keep multiple plates spinning; all in the name of work ethic. It is also a lure to numerous folks because society admires extreme hard work. Yet at the root, drivenness is rooted in a fear of not feeling good enough, not making enough money, and not being able to face the real person behind the mask, who many times is broken and afraid – the real you!

Those in the church are not exempt. Intense service and church work is admired, even if it is at the expense of the person's health and family. Inside, believers are hesitant to slow down and sit quietly before God because they are often filled with a fear that He is not pleased with them. They also fall victim of serving in ministry out of a rejection. The lie connected with this is, "If I do this work, then the church and God will be pleased with me." Yet the reality is that God wants us to serve Him through knowing and receiving His deep love for us. Yet too many serve to earn God's love and man's approval. This is a dangerous and never-ending trap. The drivenness springboards off of fear and generates a lie that our value and worth is proportionate to our productivity in this world. As a result, society strives to keep that self-accusation satisfied by working harder and longer.

A Cry for Help

In the Christian community, too many times a secure identity in the Lord is sacrificed on an altar of busyness and survival; all to keep us from facing the deep fears brewing underneath the surface. The torment continues, but many just keep going and moving, usually without stopping. Most of the time, the pattern continues until one day the person ends up in the hospital or realizes he cannot maintain sanity with the torment that has built up in his life.

This is where medication and quick fixes in the United States seem to be as common as bottled spring water. I am not an anti-medication proponent, but I feel that America has gone straight to the prescription drugs without personally dealing with the issues and torments that are causing the problems. The fact of the matter is that too many have yet to confront the issues that are laden with fear. Everyone would love to be free, yet many do not have a clue where to begin. If you are one of them, keep reading.

It breaks my heart to hear the countless stories of those who have made *vows*, which seal in the mental torment, rather than set them free. Words are spouted out in the midst of pain that vow, "I am going to make sure that I am never hurt again." This is where walls are put up which do not allow loving relationships to develop. At the same time, we engage in busyness and drivenness to keep the pain from resurfacing. In addition, the fabricated personality is immediately up for display.

Unfortunately, this person becomes unavailable for intimate connections because the lines have been cut, and the vows keep them from being spliced or reconnected. Yet the antidote—the love from God and other people—lies outside their closed-in heart. Because of a perverted outlook, love in its truest form is feared and avoided. Although individuals see themselves as being free and secured, they have actually just checked themselves into an emotional Alcatraz.

A common tactic of fear is to program its prey into running from "fearful" scenarios in order to maintain a false sense of safety. Although it starts off with a few worries or quirks, it soon escalates into a slope of anxieties and phobias. These lists begin to pile up as the escapism continues, due to fear of the future, commitment, rejection, poverty, being hurt again, death, disease and many more. I have also heard many express a struggle with even being afraid of God. Ironically, running into the arms of our Heavenly Father is the greatest way whereby we walk out of the clutches of fear.

All these coping mechanisms attempt to create a sense of safety within. Yet these habits only develop a mindset of self-preservation that will drive us to use all the resources at our disposal to keep ourselves from having to face those fears. Strong words of hurt are spoken such as, "If they don't care about me, I'm going to have to do this all on my own." Fear takes this a step further by telling us to run away.

To someone who struggles with anxiety and stress, the things that they should enjoy the most are no longer pleasurable, because the torment of fear has robbed them from being able to enjoy the simple delights God created for their enjoyment. Worse yet, people around do not have the person's full attention or his full capacity for love.

God has a design for us to be free from torment. He is not the author of it and certainly did not sadistically put any of this on us, and He has a way of victory. He desires to see us walk in freedom and wholeness. It actually hurts Him to see His children bound up in fear. Yet, no matter how deep this bondage seems, there is no wall that God cannot empower us to tear down and destroy. And as a part of this walk, God desires to build up fear's counterparts in us; faith, hope and love.

My First Hand Account

I personally understand the torment of fear. I spent many years of my life running because of fear, and I know first-hand the kind of agony fear brings.

I was involved in ministry from a very young age. Through some major events that occurred in my life, I could sense that God had a significant plan and purpose for me. As soon as I had the opportunity, I received Jesus Christ by believing in Him and the work that He did for me on the cross. I remember the day very clearly, even though I was so young; about 5 years old. I recall going to the altar with my dad to ask Jesus Christ to come into my life and save me. In my dad's own life, he had a powerful personal experience of seeing God save him from a lifestyle of drugs that had put him in jail. God got a hold of him in prison and my dad was able to get free from that destructive way of living. I can see today that a legacy of God's delivering power was being passed down into my life.

From that moment of accepting Christ into my life, the journey continued to amaze me. My dad and mom had both witnessed

God's powerful hand at work many times and I believed at a very young age that God could certainly work in signs and wonders in my life. At eight years of age I was baptized with the Holy Spirit, with the evidence of speaking in tongues at a crusade I attended with my family. No one taught me or showed me anything. The divine language came to my mouth and once again I witnessed first hand the power of God moving on my life.

With a fiery passion for the Lord, I used any opportunity I found to see God work. As a young boy, I began preaching to myself in the mirror, sharing what I learned in the Bible. Just before entering eighth grade, I responded to the call of God at a youth camp to follow after a life of full time ministry. When I was 15, I preached my first public message to my home congregation. At the age of 16 and 17, I was serving as a youth leader in my church and I also helped lead a summer discipleship program. At the time, I considered these responsibilities as significant mountains for me to climb, especially since I battled with a major fear of public speaking. Yet little did I know that the heat would be turned up a notch in my fight against fear as God would lead me to face some more amazing challenges.

Right after graduating high school, I returned home from my senior class trip, ready to work alongside my youth pastor as an intern. To my surprise, he ended up handing in his resignation one month later to serve in another church. When the news came to me, I was devastated. At the time, I was certain that God had led me to work alongside my youth pastor, and I began to wonder if He left me hanging. I struggled to know what God's next move for me would be, so in a panic I began to search for possible Bible schools to attend.

To my utter amazement, my pastor met with me and offered me a tremendous ministry opportunity — to step into leadership of our church's youth ministry! So there I was, at the age of 18, with an invitation to pastor the youth ministry of a church of about 800. I did not ask for this position, nor did I campaign for it. God sovereignly opened this door. I was fresh out of high school with no college education, yet I had a fiery passion for the Lord. I accepted the invitation and watched as God moved in power over the lives of the teenagers. In the process, I was forced to face tremendous fear and intimidation from many sides. God richly blessed and exploded the ministry, while adding many to the fellowship during those years.

About seven years later, I was invited to transition into another pastoral position in the same church; a position that involved overseeing music, worship, and church theatrical productions. This was a role for which I had not gone to school, nor had I received much formal training. I had some limited experience, but most of all, I had a heart for God and wanted so desperately for Him to move divinely in my community. So I accepted the responsibility and once again saw the Lord do mighty acts through powerful times of corporate praise and worship. Interestingly, as God was showing me how to lead the church in worship and praise, He was also working behind the scenes to break down the hidden bondage inside of me that kept me from a deep personal intimacy with God my Father.

In my own walk, I had some continual hidden torments within me that were eating away at my ability to sense God. Even though things seemed to be going pretty well in ministry, inside I was broken and terrified. On top of that, I personally lived each day as though my worth was based on the performance that I put forth in the office and on stage. Fear followed me every day to the point that I could hardly ever sit still or be quiet. Because of my lack of peace, I always felt I needed to have something to do. Moreover, I also believed that if I performed well in ministry, God would be happy and pleased with me. And I thought it to be very important to please my family and those in the congregation. Disappointing them usually led me to believe that I did something terribly wrong.

With this dysfunction came a lifestyle of drivenness and a performance mentality that was off the charts. I loved the Lord and wanted Him to touch me so deeply, yet I could not seem to grasp it because I felt I needed to earn His touch and strive for it. I became exhausted, because I felt God was always mad at me and I needed to work harder to get into His presence. I watched other people get so deeply touched by God and I always assumed it was because they prayed so much and were more spiritual than I was. I believed the more spiritual I could be, the more God would move. Yet I did not even really know what it meant to be "more spiritual."

So in a spirit of religiousness and drivenness, I attempted to get God's attention through somber prayers and more works of ministry. I would pray and pray and pray. When I felt I did not pray as much as I should, I would go into major guilt and condemnation, thinking that God was not moving because I did not pray long enough. Yet when I did pray, it never seemed to be adequate. But even during the times where I felt that I was right with God, I still felt that God was just *OK* with me. He was not thrilled with me, but He also wasn't going to kill me on the spot. Yet when I would slack, sin, or make mistakes, I felt I needed a week or so to earn my way back into decent standing with God. I believed that because I had failed and sinned, He was not pleased with me and would have to give me the silent treatment for a while.

I was riddled with fear. I feared the future. I feared church leaders. I feared my parents. I desperately feared failure and was afraid of making a wrong move that God didn't approve of, which I thought would put me out of His will. Every decision I made seemed to have an eternal destiny weighing in the balance, so I never felt free to make mistakes or to make simple choices without fear. I was convinced that one wrong move in my life would produce utter disaster. Ultimately, I was even afraid of God. I felt that He was never truly happy with me. I also could not even comprehend that He loved me in my condition. I knew He loved me enough to let me go to heaven, but not enough to let me be close to Him. I served Him diligently *for* His love, but I never served Him out of *receiving* His love.

I especially struggled deeply in being able to have relationships with the opposite sex without fear. Anytime a woman would get close, I would get into severe fear and torment over it because I never felt safe in that area. I feared having close relationships with women and I was terrified of commitment. With this in mind, I never had a very peaceful and enjoyable dating life, because I was constantly in fear and in a state of being unable to give and receive love. I deeply struggled to feel settled in letting a woman love me. In addition, my fear of rejection kept me from getting close to just about anyone.

Yet through it all, I knew deep down inside that there must be a better way. Indeed God had a much better way that He orchestrated so beautifully. As part of my pathway to freedom, God placed a prophet in the shadows into my life who walked with me and ministered to me in areas of brokenness and bondage. I was also exposed to ministries that were seeing people delivered and healed. In addition to that, I received a revelation of the Father's love that captured me so deeply and sent me on a spiritual exploration that I have never turned back from. I began to read the Bible as though for the first time. God revealed to me the traps of fear and how the devil and his kingdom author it. I also started to receive a greater level of discernment to see spiritually how fear was in operation all around me. It was at this time that a fire swelled up in my bones to help others get set free from fear through knowledge, love and authority.

Today I say with confidence that God has brought me through those painful torments and is working a process of delivering me from *all* my fears. As we will see in the rest of this book, I began to recognize what fear is, where it came from, and how to get rid of it. I have also set off on a course to know the love of God and learn what it means to know that my Heavenly Daddy loves me so very deeply. I learned that it was the love of the Father that would destroy the work of fear that sought to tear me apart. I have been walking a journey now where He is healing me and setting me free.

Today I am a married man, wed to the most wonderful woman in the world. Together we have a beautiful boy, Maximus John. My wife Melissa has loved me with a divine love that has healed many areas of brokenness in my life. Through her compassion and patience, I have been released to a greater level to defeat fear and walk as the man God intended me to be. Together, we are facing our biggest fears with victory because we are being changed and sanctified from the inside out. Years ago, I never thought I would be where I am today. I have been able to step out and face some very daunting uncertainties. Through all of these experiences, God is helping me expose fear's masquerade, revealing its pageant of lies and illusions. The pages of this book express the revelation that I came to in order to receive healing—physically and emotionally.

You are Not Crazy – You are Not Alone

I share this bring encouragement and to emphasize that you are not crazy. You are not a lunatic who belongs in an institution. You are also not the only one going through this. I know that many have told you simply to "get over it," yet you have not been able to. Fear not, for God is about to do a new work of deliverance in your life that will set you on a course to freedom. You have been attacked by an enemy that seeks to bring torment and destruction. The more you read, the greater you will see that satan is all talk. Now is the time for his secret masquerade to be revealed and for his lies to be shown in the headlines. I choose to stand in the gap with you to assure that you do not have to be bound by fear, but you can begin a process today of understanding your enemy and walking over them to victory!

I want to emphasize very clearly that fear seeks to keep us from a walk of obedient and bold *faith*. As we will see in the next chapter, fear is a counterfeit that works to drain you from being able to walk in any victorious faith. A strong faith, built into your spirit through trusting God and stepping out in obedience to Him will crush the arsenal of fear, anxiety, stress and worry.

---

[1] Matthew 6:34 (NKJV)

Chapter 6

Fear is the Perversion of Faith

. . . this is the victory that overcometh the world, even our faith.
1 John 5:4

The truth about faith and fear is that they both project to the future and demand to be engaged, valued, meditated upon and fulfilled. They equally seek for our attention and strive to be valued so that their purposes can be fulfilled in our lives. Fear and faith also both operate in an unseen realm, yet seek to manifest in this present physical reality. *The one that we choose to serve on a daily basis will be the one that becomes our visible reality.* Yet, before we move any further, let's get a deeper look at what faith is.

Faith that Destroys Fear

Now faith is the substance of things hoped for, the evidence of things not seen.
Hebrews 11:1

The word used for *faith* in this passage is the Greek word *pistis*, which speaks of a divine *conviction, reliance, constancy and assurance.* Each facet of faith's definition gives us an amazing revelation of this word, yet there is even more shown in Hebrews 11. The Scriptures speak of faith as being the *substance* of things hoped for. In other words, faith brings into our reality a world of the supernatural that cannot necessarily be perceived with the five physical senses. Faith takes from the invisible and makes it visible to those who believe and step out in obedience. Faith takes our hope, which speaks of a spiritual vision that has *confident expectation* for future events, and makes it substance. When God speaks to us, hope has the ability to be revived as we come to a greater understanding of His divine purpose for us. With that godly hope, we have a vision to look forward to and to partake in. This hope that Christ paid for is the anchor of our soul and keeps us passionately pursuing the things of God[1]. As a believer, if you have hope, there is a potential that you have faith. And when you have faith, God's message to us is to build it up, activate it and exercise it.

We have to remember that the biblical word for *hope* has a much deeper meaning than the way it is used in modern society today. Often in our culture we use the word hope as to communicate, "Man I really *hope* this works out." It is word used as a last ditch expression--that maybe if we are "lucky," something good might come out of a certain situation. It is an expression that often comes infused with much doubt and despair. Too often the word *hope* is used in contexts where people are somber, drained and looking for a last minute miracle. Yet biblical hope is so much more than that. Divine hope is *spiritual vision* — the ability to see as God sees. It is not only an anchor to our soul; hope is *joyful* anticipation, looking forward towards what you *know* God is going to do in your life.

As you read the Scriptures, it is loaded with tremendous promises that God has placed in your eternal destiny. The Holy Spirit of God takes His Word and makes it alive in us with personal application. In addition, this path and purpose is unique and creatively refreshing for each individual believer!

Our hope is in the Lord, who made heaven and earth. He created us in His image. We have a treasure within us that is working towards the good of our future. Those attacks from the enemy that come our way to try and rob us of our hope can be used as exercises to build spiritual muscle and make our anchors stronger. This hope must not be stolen, because your faith needs it to have full activation in your life.

This is too often why faith is not strong and lies dormant in the lives of people, because hope has been lost. That is why *hope deferred makes the heart sick*[2]. Hope is a fixed position; an anchor that holds us tight to a joyfully anticipated vision. When hope is alive, faith has room to operate and makes that divine hope tangible. Faith takes hope and enhances it into an assured essence and substance.

Faith shoots hope to another level by leading us to act and step forward while believing God for the fulfillment of that hope. That hope is found in Christ Jesus. Yet the evidence is not seen, which is why faith is necessary. Anything that you are pursuing that you *can* see doesn't really require faith. For example, if you are waiting for a new job in order to leave the job you know God wants you to leave, you don't need faith. In that scenario, faith means stepping out and believing for God to meet you at the next step.

Faith is necessary in the Kingdom of God because of its unseen spiritual nature. God is pleased when we are able to seek Him and walk with Him by faith,[3] which usually involves great risk and trust. Usually the greater the risk, the stronger our faith becomes. Yet this journey is not accomplished with just our five physical senses. We need faith activated into the spirit realm to pursue those things that in the natural, we cannot see. We are dealing with a supernatural world and with an unseen God who makes His activity known on earth as it is in heaven when we step out in faith.

By faith we please God[4] as seen by those who have gone before us and received a good report from God.

For by it the elders obtained a good report.
Hebrews 11:2

Godly faith unveils God's supernatural realm of the spirit to the eyes of our own spirit, so that we can operate on a level that man cannot touch or see in his own efforts. With faith, we can comprehend those things which natural man cannot even begin to know.

Through faith we understand that the worlds were framed by the word of God, so that things which are seen were not made of things which do appear.
Hebrews 11:3

Everything that we know and see on this planet was formed from the invisible world, which should encourage us as believers to realize that everything we need in our lives originates from God's invisible realm. That is why developing a life of intimacy with God by faith strengthens us, leads us and brings provision to us in abundance. It is the reason why those in Hebrews 11 were able to accomplish such great triumphs for God, because they viewed their promised hope and destiny through a spiritual lens that required faith.

Faith sees God's love and provision. Faith sees a destiny that has not yet come to pass, but recognizes that it is right around the corner. Faith looks into the future and sees God in it; therefore by that we realize there is nothing to fear.

The Counterfeit of Faith

Fear on the other hand, is the substance of things *not* hoped for, the evidence not yet seen. Fear attempts to perform the perversion of what God wants to do in your life. The Lord desires that faith be built up in you to the point that you see your future as being bright, good, and filled with hope because His Word says so. Fear on the adversarial end reminds you of the painful past and troubles and projects that doom into the future. Fear also takes new situations that lay before you and presents the worst, most dreadful results on the screen of your mind. It also encourages habits of being extra careful, paranoid and worrisome. Instead of developing a lifestyle of faith, fear demands for you to walk a lifestyle driven by anxiousness and panic.

Fear is led by satan and his kingdom to rob you of walking in freedom and godly faith. Fear is the enemy's perversion of faith in every shape and form. Like faith, fear is also unseen and presents a projected image of what could happen. Yet its projection predicts dreadful things happening. Some mistake this for intuition; not realizing that it is the enemy speaking to them.

Fear seeks to manifest its unseen realm in the natural realm here on earth by persuading people to agree with its projections. But remember, fear always projects doom, gloom, and dreadful results. Fear never projects a positive hope filled with success and security.

Faith from God reveals that you are a loved, highly favored child of God with a tremendous hope and future.

In all honesty, I want to truly get to the place in my life, where the majority of my decisions, thought processes, and dreams are guided by my faith and trust in God, not fear. If we all became transparently honest with ourselves, there would probably be an admittance that we all live way too much of our lives based on fear rather than on faith. We've paid way too much attention to the video projections that fear has presented, and its time for a change. Your freedom over fear and your wholeness is going to greatly depend on how you change your ways of handling what is projected into your spirit and soul. Will you develop a lifestyle of faith that projects hope and a solid purpose that is sure, or will you continue to watch what fear has playing in the theatre?

The wonderful news is that God has a much better way for us to walk in. God is waiting patiently for you and me to step out of situations that have been guided by fear and place our trust in Him. Surrender is really a key component, because it releases God to work to a greater extent in our lives, while causing us to enter in greater rest. Our Father is speaking to His people today, that if they would release more to Him (that is, hand over control, the daily burdens and cares) it would release more of His presence and power in their communities. He truly is a faithful Father that desires to take us by the hand and lead us. Faith *leads*. Fear *drives*.

Faith Leads

Psalm 23 is a wonderful example of how God leads His children along in life. It says in His Word that He *"leads* me beside the still waters." It is important to notice here that God is shown in this passage as a wonderful Shepherd. A shepherd understands the sheep that are in his care, and he will go out of his way to insure the safety and health of the flock. His desire is to lead the sheep into places of peace and rest. As long as the shepherd is there, everything is OK.

The word *lead* in the original language actually means "to run with a sparkle, flow, protect, sustain, carry, feed, guide, lead (gently, on)." That is a powerful expression He is using for us here!

God is saying that He is *running with a sparkle*, probably because He loves us so much as our Daddy and is excited beyond human comprehension at our existence and potential. He is protecting us, sustaining us, carrying us, feeding us, guiding us, and gently showing us a place of rest. Psalm 23:2a could read, "He *causes* us to lie down in green pastures." That is what God will do for His sheep, His children! It is God's desire for you! If only we would release ourselves to let God do just that.

In Hebrews 4, God proclaims His call for His people to be led into that place that He refers to as "rest." It is a place that every believer needs to strive to enter. Interestingly enough, there is pretty much nothing that God wants us striving in or becoming driven about, yet He makes an exception here in Hebrews. The instructions are clear. The only area where it is acceptable in the Kingdom to be driven is when we *daily strive to enter into His rest.* Basically in the spirit, we are told to wake up, run and hustle to go rest! What a concept! This is the arena where God's Kingdom is unleashed. It's not a position void of activity. It doesn't mean sitting on the couch all day waiting for things to happen. It's an active position of release and surrender, allowing God to guide and direct us, while He takes care of the results. This is your daily assignment to enter into His rest.

It seems like a contradiction in teaching, but it is not man's doctrine, it is Kingdom teaching. We enter that place of rest through our belief and trust that He is our Good Shepherd who will take special care of those who put themselves under His care.

Fear Drives

I find that God's faith has a unique way of *leading* us, not driving us. God does not drive us and force us, but He guides us sovereignly to paths of righteousness and to destinations of supernatural greatness. Yet fear has a way of driving you, pushing you, and relentlessly hurrying you to do all you can to survive, strive and escape. But if we look back at Hebrews 4, we see that there is a process of patience, waiting, and letting go that needs to take place.

For he that is entered into his rest, he also hath ceased from his own works,
as God did from his.
Hebrews 4:10

In order to receive freedom from fear, we have to repent of and let go of drivenness and striving; of constantly being hurried and carrying burdens we ought to not carry. God has not called us to be false-burden bearers, nor has He called us to strive to earn Kingdom results. He has called us to enter into rest while casting *all* our cares upon Him, because He cares for us.

It is time that we cease from our own works: the works that we have jumped into; the works that we have attributed to God that He never told us to do; the works that do nothing but add more stress, anxiety and frustration. It is time that we run into His rest and let His Holy Spirit gently guide and direct our steps. I have found that when I have done this, God's hands brought exponential results more than I ever could have mustered up in ten lifetimes.

When I served on a church staff, I had all sorts of projects that I strived through. Many times I justified that drivenness and gave credit to God for all of it. Now I certainly do not take away from the wonderful ways that God used me during those seasons. There were certainly some awesome things He did through me. Yet in retrospect, He just wanted me to rest in Him more; not add more meetings and perform more tasks. He wanted my extra time to be filled with rest, enjoyment, and fellowship with His presence and His people. He wanted me to lovingly share the gospel with all who would hear and receive. He desired for me to lay down all my dead works and let His Spirit lead the way to bring about supernatural increase.

I wanted to please Him with my efforts, yet He was already pleased with me. He just wanted me to rest in Him. I am not teaching against working hard or being diligent. Discipline and hard work is wonderful, but let us go to God's higher level of surrender, where we can work hard, yet be at rest inside. It is what makes room for God to accomplish supernatural things in our lives. Striving and drivenness are based on fear. Faith is based on rest and hope found in Christ Jesus.

Faith in Action

Many who struggle with fear have a really tough time discerning the voice of God. Too much pressure has been placed upon them to try and figure through all the voices that clamor for their attention. I believe that by unveiling fear's tactics, you can move from being driven by fear to being led by the Spirit of God. This will take some time, practice, renewal and some deliverance, but through divine understanding and the power of Jesus Christ, it can be done.

God's Holy Spirit does not drive us, but leads us in the paths of God's will and desire. Fear pushes and drives incessantly from the back seat screaming, "Common let's go! You'd better do this now! You'd better hurry! Go! Go! Hurry! Hurry! Worry! Worry! What if? What if? What are you going to do now?" With all those impulses and bombardments too many people end up exhausted and burned out at the end of the day. They lose their resources and wonder why they are fried, tense, stressed out, depressed, and sick. It's because we have allowed fear to drive us instead of faith leading us.

Would you like to live in a better way? Let's start by asking God to help us develop our faith through entering into His rest. Remember, to everyone God has given a measure of faith,[5] which means that no matter where you are, you have something to start with. All you need is the faith the size of a mustard seed, so don't get into believing this is something you have to work up. It is actually a practice of resting; a process of stepping out in trust, while releasing ourselves into His care. (We will cover this more in chapters ahead.)

Yet at the same time, we have to go a little deeper, because for millions of people, the assignment of building up faith has been difficult and challenging, because they are *brokenhearted*. This leads us to understand why great faith has not been developed in many and why fear has taken the place of faith in the lives of millions. This next chapter will delve into why this is occurring as we look into the void that allows fear to bring torment.

[1] Hebrews 6:18-19
[2] Proverbs 13:12
[3] Hebrews 11:6
[4] Hebrews 11:6
[5] Romans 12:3

Chapter 7

He Who Fears Lacks Perfecting Love

*And we have known and believed the love that God has for us. God is love,
and he who abides in love abides in God, and God in him. Love has been
perfected among us in this: that we may have boldness in the day of
judgment; because as He is, so are we in this world. There is no fear in
love; but perfect love casts out fear, because fear involves torment. But he
who fears has not been made perfect in love. We love Him because He first
loved us.*
1 John 4:16-19 (NKJV)

If you show me anyone who struggles with stress, anxiety and
worry at increased levels or even low doses, I will also show you
someone who has not been perfected in love, especially in the area
that fear is attacking. It is usually a guarantee that this person has a
personal history of not being loved, covered and nurtured properly
in their life. Because of lack and emptiness, fear takes advantage.
Wherever there is a void of love, there is usually a root of fear
seeking to sprout.

A trail of "lovelessness" begins for many in the developing
period of childhood. It is at this stage that we are most vulnerable
to fear, especially when we need love and nurturing as a part of our
foundational development. The vulnerability to fear grows when
love, acceptance and covering are absent. Many homes are filled
with rage, strife, and quarreling, leaving a wide open door for fear
to pull in and initiate its tormenting oppressions. Other homes can
seem fulfilled, yet underneath the surface lays a hidden
undercurrent of performance pressures, drivenness mentalities, and

perfectionist ambitions. These excessively high standards, if pushed with too much intensity and pressure, can create fountains of potential distress and anxiety in the lives of family members. The point is, fear always looks for an area where love is absent so it can utilize its weapons.

Hearing the Words, "I Love You"

The word *love* contains such depth; its meaning is so profound, especially when expressed from the heart. One of the most dominant ways that love is spread throughout our world is through the power of spoken words. When released from a heart filled with compassion in a timely moment, the words, "I love you" can add a sense of safety, empowerment, and care like nothing else. Love's verbalization is certainly most impacting from our parents and guardians, who raise us, speak over us and have tremendous weight in the development of our lives. Yet for the multitudes struggling with fear, there is no memory of receiving the words, "I love you" from a father or a mother. These three words spoken frequently and backed with loving actions build an internal compass within human beings to ward off the threat of fear's attacks. Unfortunately, the number of people who do not even understand this blessing in their life is growing in these generations and has not shown any signs of decreasing.

As a child, we all cling tightly to the words our parents speak to us and we observe their actions with a great deal of learning. The initial experiences impart values and foundations that are laid to build a growing future. When love is largely absent or conditional, it can create a deep-seated wound where fear can become a greater factor. This truth is not intended to induce any guilt or additional pain in our life, but it is given to help us simply recognize that there were some hurts and significant areas where love was lacking. Most people who have experienced this in their life have turned into warriors, telling their world that everything is fine and all is well. They have lived with a tough exterior in attempts to fool others that they are "over it." While deep in their heart is a brokenness that desperately needs to be mended. It is at this place where the healing work of God's love can mend undercurrents of brokenness which keep men and women in bondage — especially to fear.

The Father Image

I served in youth ministry as a youth worker and later as a pastor for over 10 years, during which I witnessed great numbers of teenagers manifest the results of not being shown love in their families. In that season of ministry, I was amazed at how often I interacted with believing teens that did not truly have a revelation of the love of God, especially as their Father in Heaven. I related to their struggles because I wrestled with that understanding myself.

Throughout my times of preaching, teaching and ministry I would attempt to communicate the love of their Heavenly Father to them. These attempts many times would induce nothing more than a blank stare and empty expressions. Many would respond back to me by saying, "Mark, you want me to call Him my Heavenly Father? Are you kidding me?" There was an internal disconnect of seeing God through that lens because of the dysfunction they lived through. They learned to see a "father" as someone to be scared of, someone who was not around, or a man in the house who was emotionally disconnected. The title, "Daddy" was not a pleasurable association. Yet God's original design was for *Daddy* to be an image that reflects the love, care and covering of our Father in Heaven.

God Created Relationships For Us to Know His Love

It is very important that we understand that God created human relationships so we could have a visible, tangible representation of His love and care for us. He is a relational God who determined to reveal His identity of love through human relationships and heart to heart interactions here on earth. When you grow up receiving love from your earthly father, you are given a tangible image of your Heavenly Father's love. When love, nurture and care is bestowed on you from your earthly mother, the nurturing of the Lord is revealed and established through an earthen vessel. As one develops and matures, the framework of learning to give and receive love in friendships and relationships is developed.

When a couple enters into a long term loving relationship of romance and commitment, that pathway usually leads to a marriage. This godly institution was established by God to give us an earthly representation of Christ's relationship to the church. When a husband loves his wife as Christ loves the church, He will do anything to make sure that his spouse is loved and cared for in every decision that he makes. She is put first and is second only to God. In addition, when a wife submits to her husband, this action reveals the opportunity that we all have to submit ourselves under the covering and protection of a loving Almighty God. As God is a covering to us, so should a man cover his wife. When the journey continues in marriage, usually children enter into the picture. As this stage unfolds, the cycle comes full circle as parents have the privilege of imparting love and godly character to sons and daughters who will carry on a legacy. It was God's blueprint from the beginning to have these relationships equip people in understanding their identity and for fulfilling their life purpose.

The Bible says that God is love. He doesn't just *have* love. He *is* love. God is the very essence of love. When you see or experience love in this world, you have witnessed God. This love is so powerful that it can extend to the entire world. When someone experiences the blessings of a loving parent or relationship, that connection is a gift from Father God. The fascinating thing is that you do not even have to be a Christian to experience that blessing. That is just how loving God is! He created love to the point that even unbelievers can experience these blessings.

Every time someone experiences love here on earth, they receive a blessing from God. Additionally, anyone who has received a distorted dose of love, or has been dealt a perversion of love has experienced something that is *not* from God. Let us make sure we get that straight and clear. *You were designed and intended by God to enter into a world where you are loved, accepted and cherished.* Anything other than that is a counterfeit and not God's desire. He is not the author of that pain nor is He the reason behind it. In fact, it hurts His heart to see injustice and trauma brought on to His children. These dreadful experiences are the result of people making wrong choices, while giving in to an enemy kingdom of thought processes and actions that are contrary to the knowledge of God.

Not to Blame, But to Forgive

This is not intended to put blame and shame on your parents and guardians who were responsible to love you, nor is it meant to send people into a spiral of self-pity and endless hopelessness. It is brought to the surface in order to reveal a reality of serious hurt and pain that gave the enemy room to bring oppression to you and communicate that you are less than special and wonderful. This reality is also being addressed to those who have lived their lives as tough soldiers, yet underneath are brokenhearted souls who need healing. In addition, the wounds of the past may be good to deal with so that appropriate forgiveness and potential reconciliation can take place. This truly gives people an opportunity to begin to move on from the past that is keeping them from a promising future.

In most cases, past hurts, pains, disappointments and pressures bring great dysfunction into the present reality. Allow me to give some basic illustrations as to how this happens. Oftentimes, those who struggle with a *fear of poverty* grew up in a home where there was a heavy financial struggle and where the fear of becoming poor was emphasized. Those who struggle with a fear of rejection were most likely rejected significantly at some stage in their life. Unfortunately they end up living their life trying to prove they are something, while at the same time living in panic of being rejected again. Those who push away form being intimate with loving people have probably experienced a perverted view of love. They end up living and working to keep any threat of being unloved away, yet at the same time they miss out on truly being loved and accepted.

Because of all this, scores of generations end up seeing the same sins and patterns of their parents repeated in their own life, even without direct teaching or examples. That is the nature of spiritual oppression and sin: to destroy entire legacies. With this tragedy, we end up with spiritually and mentally dysfunctional patterns that repeat themselves in families with compounding force.

This is why the message of the Father's love seeks to hit the core of wounded hearts. Too many traumas have never been healed, victimizations have not been addressed and long-term fears have been masked over. The love of God is seeking to invade our communities which desperately need it. Our society is manifesting a deep seated emptiness that needs His love to invade our lives like never before.

My heart is crying out to see this generation make a break this bondage of fear. I believe this will explode to a greater dimension when a wide spread renewal of Father God's love hits our regions and nations. That love is like a fire burning within my heart. I have a vision to see the nations set free as God's love brings deliverance and healing. Through knowing God and His love intimately, those under the clutches of fear will begin to run free in liberty. I believe it is time that we allow God to heal our broken hearts and allow His Spirit to break the power of fear. Why not give the enemy an eviction notice to let him know we will not be tormented anymore!

Who's Got Your Back?

Our leverage against fear many times comes down to a very simple question: *Who's got my back?* The answer to this question either sends people into despair and fear, or into a safe rest of confidence and peace. Many times you can tell just by looking into the faces of certain people—that someone, somewhere down the line in the past *had their back* on many occasions. Usually it is a loved one like a parent, brother or person who stepped into that kind of role. God's intended design was for us to have relationships that would be a covering during periods of hardship and struggle. This was purposed to reflect the faithfulness and comfort that God brings.

Our parents were the ones intended to the first to *have our back*. They were intended to be available to help us navigate through our tests and trials, while eventually releasing us off our training wheels so we can independently maneuver through life with confidence. Those training times placed in us a compass of assurance, knowing that if things do not work out, somebody will surely come and bring aid in that time of need.

Yet this does not end after teen years. There are seasons we all enter that are extremely unfamiliar, where godly mentoring and wise advice breathe life into us. In addition, this support is equipping us to go out and take on the world with our dreams. In the end, we know that someone will be there for us if certain decisions do not work out.

Although our hope is truly in the Lord alone, He uses these earthly relationships to help us understand how faithful He is. It helps the lenses of our development focus on the love and security we have in God, with the expectation of leading us into personal intimacy with Him. His love and faithfulness are strewn all throughout Scripture.

As a father has compassion on his children, so the LORD has compassion on those who fear him.
Psalms 103:13 (NIV)

. . . for he hath said, I will never leave thee, nor forsake thee.
So that we may boldly say, The Lord is my helper, and I will not fear what man shall do unto me.
Hebrews 13:5b-6

Knowing that God *has our back* is learned many times through those who represent His love and faithfulness to us. Yet when that is not properly demonstrated, our view of God becomes distorted and the enemy can take advantage by tormenting us. This is why we must recognize that in the area that we are vulnerable to fear, we have not yet been perfected in love. Truly knowing that God loves you sends clear signals to your inner man that there is nothing to fear. The awesome fact is that God can turn around those areas and even use you to help others receive God's love and extend it to others. If God loves us and He is our helper, what can *anyone* do to us?

Be Perfected in Love

To anyone who struggles with fear, let me help lay out a journey that will take your healing and freedom from fear to a stronger level. The exhortation for you is to walk a journey of understanding love in the way God designed it, not in a perverted way or in a conditional sense. Understanding love in your heart is intended to lead you to God, and understanding God in His love will lead to freedom. Your journey will entail receiving a personal revelation of the love of God the Father.

The reality is that most of our problems stem from not understanding and receiving the love of God. In any area where there is fear, lies an area that has not yet been perfected in love. When we sin and live out of an area of bondage, we are not just sinning against God; we are running away from His love and faithfulness. If we truly know that He loves us deeply, the running will stop and we will come home; home to a love that can be experienced.

Of course, receiving His love is not simply a cerebral process, but one that must be engaged with the heart. Out of this seat of affection is where God can have a pivot point to move in all areas of our life. A surrendered heart trusts in the love of God so much that full release into His care becomes possible. As we give permission for Him to move in our heart, healing can take place as the Father's love drives out the power of fear.

This supreme power of love does not just apply to fear alone; it reveals a powerful force of deliverance from any kind of bondage or stronghold in our life. Receiving a revelation of God's true love can break the powers of rejection, bitterness, hardness of heart, self-hatred, unforgiveness and many other areas. Those who struggle with addictions of any kind have a deep root of absent love. They carry a sign on their heart that says "Desperate Need to Be Loved!" Yet those bound with addictions attempt to fulfill that lack in ways that only give them a temporary and perverted "high", leading them to further bondage.

We Want to Know that We are Loved and Safe

Inside the hearts of human beings lies a capsule that was designed to be filled with God's love. The truth about this capsule is that if the love of God does not fill it, the heart will long for a supply that usually comes from a polluted or diluted source. A heart in search of meaning, belonging and love will sometimes search to the ends of the world to find fulfillment.

When a person is this vulnerable, many weapons of the enemy can enter, including the weapons of fear: anxiety, stress, worry, and panic. When fear comes in, it will use anything in its arsenal to get people to live a driven lifestyle rather than one led by love. In addition, people with fear will feel they need to earn any love they can get. So what we end up with is populations of broken people who do not know *why* they are doing what they are doing. Yet God knows that there is a void inside of them that has not been touched by His tender hand of love. It is a love that has good things in store for us and a message that says there is nothing to be afraid of.

This battle against fear is made clearer as we understand that fear, anxiety, stress and worry do *not* come from God. They originate from another kingdom that has no desire to see you walk in freedom and love.

Chapter 8

Fear Is Not From God

For God has not given us the spirit of fear . . . **2 Timothy 1:7**

On the authority of God's Word, I can freely tell you this with complete confidence: ***tormenting fear does not come from God.*** Let this truth become a personal revelation as it sinks deeply into your heart and brings illumination and peace. For me, receiving this realization in my heart brought a sense of peace that breathed fresh air into my life. Allow the Holy Spirit to remind you of this when fear is knocking on your door: it is not from Him.

It is Not God

As simple as it seems, this thought is something that many fail to utilize in their battle against fear. Your first line of defense when fear rears its ugly head is that you can say with great assurance, "This is not from God!" God is consumed with how much He loves us, not by how he can sadistically torment us, yet many are still perplexed on this matter. Fear is not in His nature nor does He use it to speak to people or motivate them. From that understanding, we have an advantage against our enemy's deception with a greater level of discernment.

Too many Christians get confused in their war against their spiritual enemy because they blame God for calamities He never sent and they give Him credit for fears that He did not send. God designed the "fight or flight" response system in our bodies, but He did not intend for it to be abused by stress and tormenting anxiety. His desire is for us to walk in faith, hope, love and peace.

Too many blame God for their anxiety, panic and even sickness. Because so many are struggling to obtain victory over fear, they end up saying that God put it on them to teach them something. They end up changing their beliefs based on their lack of triumph over fear. In the end, God's character and power are compromised and diluted in their lives.

God is not the author of evil, nor does He tempt humanity with evil. God loves the entire planet. Before we ever loved Him, He loved us so much that He sent His Son to die. It is imperative that we do not disgrace His character by blaming fear and anxiety attacks that come our way upon God. He is a loving Father who only wants good things for His children.

It is also important to remember that God has certainly placed us into a spiritual battlefield to establish His kingdom on earth as it is in heaven. As a part of this battle, fear presents itself as one of our foes. The good news is that God through Christ Jesus has given us the spiritual weapons and artillery to stand up against this adversary and defeat it. In addition to spiritual authority, God has given us His all encompassing and unconditional love that has the power to cast out fear and its effects. Unfortunately, too many souls have lost the battle against fear at the starting gate because they do not even know who their enemy is and they have become ignorant of satan's devices.

God's Role of Recompense and Justice

God is *not* the author of fear, anxiety, stress and worry. Not only that, He does not like to see His children bound by it. He looks over His creation as a loving Father who actually wants to see His sons and daughters free from its grip. God does not take delight in seeing any of His people live in hopelessness or torment and He has a better way. He was not a part of that abuse that came to your home. God was not the author of those anxious environments you grew up in. He was not pleased to see that person victimize you. I plead with you to not blame Him, because those calamities are not a part of His ways.

Yet through all this, God has a way of turning those wounds around for your spiritual advancement. He has a redemptive plan that involves reconciliation, recompense and justice in our lives. The Scriptures tell us that God loves justice.[1] In addition, He requires the thief to return seven fold what was stolen.[2] With that said, it is important to know first of all that God did not bring those fears upon you. He has a divine plan to set you free and bring back that which was stolen from you with interest! All those medical bills you paid, those wasted days in worry and the relational issues you suffered through can be brought back in compounding effect. God's order of divine justice has a powerful way of redeeming those things which were lost.

The Lord's desire is not only to set you free, but to see you walk in what I like to call, "spiritual payback." This principle comes into play when we begin to take back ground that was stolen by the enemy through walking in victory over fear and leading others towards freedom.

I am unwrapping this concept at this stage in the book to help implant a vision within you, of where you are headed. As fear's armor is dismantled, the Kingdom of God can redeem those areas formerly plagued with fear by imparting boldness, love, clarity of mind and power in your life. With this principle, God has a way of bringing back those things that were taken during times of anxiety and worry; from financial loss to lost time and sanity. Not only has this become a part of my personal journey, it is something that I am spiritually contending for.

Removing Fear's Ability to Speak

I have found that simply understanding that God was not sending anxiety and worry at me was crucial in my journey because it accelerated the process of showing what God was *not* saying, so it helped me to discern what He *was and is* saying. Cultivating this discernment can also divinely reveal who you are *not*, so that you can discover who God says you *are*. For those who want to truly hear God's voice, many times it can begin with refusing to give ear to the promptings of fear so your Heavenly Father can speak in His love and power. Knowing when fear is knocking on your door can aid in keeping its torment out, as well as help to bring clarity and alignment within you to receive the voice of God.

This is imperative because in all honesty, too much fear is influencing the actions and decisions of people. They have misunderstood the voice of fear as being wisdom or even the voice of the Lord. We have to remember that God does not speak in a voice of tormenting fear. Fear, anxiety, stress and worry are not a part of His character nor are they an ingredient of His workings. God's Word communicates that He offers every believer power, love and a sound mind.[3] Yet instead of power, fear produces immobility, passiveness and timidity. Rather than soaking in love, fear drives you to escape, panic and isolate. When fear is in operation, you can forget having a sound mind, because it will never offer it. Torment, terror, anxiety, dread, worry, panic, and insanity become the atmospheric conditions. When fear is in command, there is a struggle to even have strength and motivation. Let us diligently seek to listen to the voice of power, love and sound thinking.

Fear is Not a Part of Your Design

When fear is stirring up, recognize this principle: God does not see you as a fearful person. His vision of you from the foundation of the earth does not include fear as a part of your personal blueprint. His plan and design is for you to become conformed into the image of His Son while viewing yourself as a joint heir with Jesus Christ.[4] Your identity is a son or daughter of the Most High God. He is your Father and Daddy, and out of that identity He desires for you to freely live and move and have your being.[5] For each of you as individuals, God has unique and powerful assignments that He wants to send you to fulfill. From His heart, He will impart to you a strong sense of boldness, confidence, faith and love in addition to the giftings He has put inside you. Of course, fear will seek to keep you from stepping out into that assignment with every weapon in its arsenal. So a part of God's plan involves us overcoming fear and stepping out into our spiritual destiny. As we align ourselves in this truth, our objective turns to seeking to be who God wants us to be, not what fear has programmed us to be.

Once you recognize these things, you will start to see that *you are not fear*. When fear is kicking up in any shape or form, remember that it is not you! This might seem to be too simple of a concept, but for many, fear has shaped and designed their personalities. We will end up describing ourselves in terms of the fears working within us if we are not exercised in spiritual discernment. You are *not* a fearful person, an anxious person, or a worrier. You are not a timid person, nor are you a shy person. He has called you to be a chosen generation and a royal priesthood; called out of darkness and into His marvelous light. You are also called to *proclaim* the praises of Him Who called you out.[6] How are you going to do that if you are driven into the corner with fear and trepidation? How do we honestly represent God in this world as kings and priests if we are up to our ears in fear? This identity description certainly does not describe someone who is driven and bound by fear. It is not a part of your destined identity.

Too Good To Be True?

I know for many of you, this may seem like "pie in the sky" thinking, yet it is simple and foundational truth from Scripture. Fear is a spirit from Satan's kingdom that you need to take your rightful place against. It has entered territory that it does not belong in and this trespassing needs to be reckoned with. Once you begin to separate the work of fear as being something that is *not* you and not from God, it clarifies vision and discernment, allowing you to be more mindful of Satan's tactics.

I can remember time and time again, as I was learning to defeat anxiety and panic attacks, I would remind myself, "This is not from God and this is *not* me. This is from the enemy." Fear had come against me and I was determined to win the battle over it. Time and time again I would repeat this until I understood fully in my heart and mind that it was true. With this practice, I gradually began to build an arsenal that would eventually avalanche the fortress of fear.

Bringing Clarity to the Stress

How often have you noticed that many of the things you have worried about or spent endless times in anxiety over never really came to pass? Yet even though they do not come to pass, we still do not seem to get true victory when the storm passes. As soon as one storm passes, we start to focus on the doom and gloom of the next obstacle.

A solid example of this in Mark 6, where Jesus breaks the fear of lack of provision by feeding five thousand people with five loaves and two fish. You see, when God activates a miracle of provision, it is not just demonstrated to meet a need, but also to manifest the glory of God and move us to a greater level of faith. The divine works of God naturally push back the works of the enemy, especially fear.

After the miracle of the loaves, the disciples found themselves in a wild storm. Jesus in fact saw them in a vision, struggling to row against the wind that was pounding against them. So He steps out and walks on the water towards the boat. The disciples, who were not quite trained to expect the supernatural, thought that Jesus was a ghost. Our Lord stepped into the boat and brought peace and calmness to the waters.

The amazing revelation comes in Mark 6:51-52, which reveals the difficulty the disciples had in being able to enter into a fearful storm with greater authority and peace.

And he went up unto them into the ship; and the wind ceased: and they were sore amazed in themselves beyond measure, and wondered. For they considered not the miracle of the loaves: for their heart was hardened.
Mark 6:51-52

Each time God brings a victory over fear in our lives, those events need to be supernatural benchmarks that remind of us of our destiny towards freedom. Just as David reminded himself of past victories as he faced looming obstacles, you and I need to focus on the good things that God has done while setting our eyes on the great works He is going to perform in the future. And as a part of that divine purpose and vision, God does not have fear as a contributing part of the equation.

---

[1] Isaiah 61:8 (NKJV)
[2] Proverbs 6:31
[3] 2 Timothy 1:7
[4] Romans 8:16-17

[5] Acts 17:28
[6] 1 Peter 2:9

Chapter 9

Fear is Not You

Now if I do what I do not want to do, it is no longer I who do it, but it is sin living in me that does it.
Romans 7:20 (NIV)

As we reveal the true nature of fear, it is important that we understand its identity from God's perspective. The truth from this chapter has the power to release a great deal of freedom when it is digested into our inner man and applied to daily living.

God's Command: Fear Not

Fear is not from God and it is not a part of the nature you have in Christ. Fear's nature is sin. From beginning to end, the Scriptures clearly reveal God commanding His people to "fear not." In fact the Word of God tells us specifically to "fear not" about as many times as there are days in a year! It is one of the predominant phrases that is repeated consistently in the Bible; and it is often directed towards people whom God wanted to use greatly.

Almighty God knew we would have to face fear so He commanded us repeatedly *not* to give in to it. He gave people the task of climbing enormous mountains—all they had to do was not fear. God equips us with great power over the enemy's devices—we simply need not fear. We are told in His Word to step out in faith without fear. Yet it is amazing how many times we disobey that heavenly command because we do not trust Father God's care over us and we fail to rest in His love.

Fear's Tactic: Remove Trust and Faith in God

To put it very bluntly, *fear is a lack of trusting in God.* It communicates that God has forgotten us and will not be there to help in the time of need. The bottom line message that fear communicates is that God is not capable of being trusted with issues that we concern ourselves with. Fear says that God will not come through in your life and will not protect you in your circumstances. Fear calls God a liar and tells us to take matters into our own hands. Fear works to convince us that the obstacle or problem in front of us is greater than the God you serve.

Fear's Nature: Sin

The Bible says in Romans that whatever is not of faith is sin[1]. The body of Christ has carelessly forgotten this truth, but has also avoided this thought of fear being sin because of the legalistic teachings they have been exposed to. Well meaning leaders and teachers who were tainted with legalism, condemnation and religiousness screamed at people about their sins. Instead of being focused on love and graciously helping people towards freedom, they were always *sin conscious.* With that dysfunctional focus, they were always looking for sin in people's lives and would condemningly beat them into submission and conformity.

Yet what it brought was more bondage as the love of God and His grace were rarely demonstrated. God's love that brought Jesus to die was given many times to people conditionally, only when they were "clean" and "holy." The problem was that the standards of holiness were mostly man made and lacked love. Too many in the church unlovingly harassed people about sin, while failing to recognize their own hypocrisy and iniquity. In addition, the power of God's love and grace was not appropriated in its fullest power.

My word of exhortation and awakening is not a message of condemnation. Please do not receive this chapter as a legalistic punch. This also is not a word intended to ignite additional fear into your life either. Too many who do not understand grace and love end up keeping a constant search for what sin may be in their lives, often leading them to greater bondage. This chapter is simply a reality from God's Word that we *all* have to deal with. We all have areas of fear that we need victory over and we have no reason to feel judged or condemned (those thoughts are not from God). Let this actually be a word of love and grace, leading you to greater *freedom*. We all need to be transparent and come together, recognizing our servitude to sin in the area of fear and make the decision to help each other break through. With that mindset, we can acknowledge in unity that fear has been used against God's people for far too long and it is time we walk into victory!

People are Looking for Answers

The inability for society to get victory over fear has driven many in mass numbers to seek help from counselors, psychologists, psychiatrists and all sorts of practitioners. I am certainly not against these modes of help, but unfortunately too many therapy models both in and outside the church have blended themselves with teachings of psychotherapy. These modalities, though well intentioned, have led people down paths of confusion and even greater bondage; sometimes in the name of the Lord. If we are not discerning, these methods will contaminate the delivering power of the Gospel; watering down its ability to set people free.

Even the church has struggled to bring freedom from fear to the body. As a result, countless lives are endeavoring to find other practices and techniques, many of which can lead people astray and pose danger. Yet because humanity is so desperate for answers, they will search endlessly for solutions to their fear issues. Many times this leads them to avenues that promise to alleviate pain and bring help, but are rooted in deception and bondage.

For example, if you carefully trace the history of countless counseling and therapy models, you will find many of these practices rooted in the ideas and philosophies of men like Sigmund Freud and Carl Jung.[2] These teachings have taken on new names and have certainly evolved, but nonetheless are being used today as resources to help to people. Richard Noll, a clinical psychologist wrote about the practices and teachings of Carl Jung:

Carl Jung was openly hostile to Judeo-Christian orthodoxies . . . however, we increasingly find Protestants, Catholics, and Jews adopting alternative beliefs systems that often belie a basis on Jungian "psychological" theories . . . I make this judgment about Jung without being either Christian or Jew or Moslem – or Freudian.[3]

Even though we as a church seem to lay claim to standing upon biblical principles, we find ourselves straining to reach and pull from external philosophies, techniques, and teachings, mostly because we are not witnessing the freedom the Scriptures say we can have. As a result, church doctrine and theology have been modified over the years to match this lack of biblical experience. This spiritual void ought to lead us to re-evaluate our ways and ask God to revive His Word in us once again. We have failed to recognize our errors in scriptural interpretations and understandings, which if acknowledged, would lead us to revisit God's Word in establishing a more firm foundation. Instead, churches have turned to the practitioners of the world to help them do what God through Christ Jesus equipped the church to accomplish, which is to bring the full gospel of salvation, healing and deliverance to those in captivity.

Tracing the Roots

Much of the history of psychology deals with the journey of man attempting to deal with inner struggles and dysfunctional behavior through experimental therapy models and deep inner reflection. Carl Jung, a psychiatrist from Switzerland, is in many circles considered the founder of analytical psychology.

From the early years, documented writings speak of the torment and unsettled experiences that Mr. Jung underwent. Even in childhood, Carl Jung felt inside that he had two personalities[4]. Through his journey to find answers and experiential research, he came to some very "enlightening" experiences; mostly which the Bible speaks of as the body of sin and evil spirits who perpetuate sin. He certainly did not want to name demonics as evil spirits, so instead, those spirits he encountered were named "complexes", while the realm they operated in were named "the unconscious". The unconscious was considered to be a domain within where human ancestral darkness resides.[5]

In addition to these terms, Jung also coined the word "shadow," which was used to describe everything that a person does not want to acknowledge about himself that lie below conscious thinking. This has even influenced our current culture, which uses this term *shadow* in reference to a subconscious arena of the mind.

Even personality profiles that include the *extrovert* and *introvert* categories, which are used all around the world, trace their steps back to Jung's teachings. His philosophies led people to believe that both of these personality traits existed in every person and needed to be balanced out in life. The term "archetype" was taught in relation to the shadow and subconscious teachings; speaking of an inherited idea or way of thinking that is present in the unconsciousness of an individual. All these terms referred to areas of dysfunction and evil that created struggle within people.

Sigmund Freud, an Austrian psychiatrist, has also greatly affected modern thinking through his research, theories, and development of the psychoanalytic school of psychology. Freud had similar terminology that he coined to name the place of inner struggle and dysfunction. He called it the "unconscious mind" where the "beast" within us resides. Many other philosophers and teachers, including Jung, used similar concepts, with a few terms being slightly altered or changed.

A Greater Antidote

Yet many in history have failed to personally realize that the identification and solution to the whole matter of dealing with the evil within is actually laid out in the totality of the Scriptures.

In modern psychology, through a process of integration and continual therapy, one is taught to come to a place of living with this world of the collective unconscious, archetypes, dark shadows, personality traits and other areas. Yet the problem is that these techniques and philosophies never truly help someone to get free of anxiety, depression, and fear related issues — or any struggle for that matter.

For those who engage this process of integration, many only come to a place of greater torment and double mindedness because they attempt to make friends with an evil kingdom that seeks to destroy them. For most, the only solution left to alleviate the insanity within eventually becomes a pathway of prescription drugs or natural remedies of some kind to cover the pain or alleviate symptoms. That is why we live in a world where humanity will try anything to find that inner peace, including occultic new age pathways, alternative medicine, illegal and legal drugs, and various addictions.

Who Determines Our Identity?

The teaching of personality profiles has really intrigued me, because of the cultural fascination that exists where *people seem to love to label others.* There is such a common habit to quickly jump and label people into a certain category, thus boxing them into a limited potential. When we do this, we fail to keep the vast expanse of possibilities open to that person's life. For example, when we see that a teenager has a hard time being able to socialize in larger crowd settings, we tend to quickly label that young person as being *shy.*

I personally find that the introvert/extrovert, shy/outgoing conversation would not be up for as much discussion if we truly attacked fear in our families and communities and cut it off at the knees. If we all become truly honest with ourselves, we will find that introversion is mainly a fear-based issue. You take fear out of the picture, and it is a guarantee that you will not hear anyone saying that they are passive, shy, introverted, timid, or reserved.

I say this with all due love and respect, but nowhere in Scriptures can you see God adding those traits to His description of us. He calls us to be bold, to proclaim His praises, and not to be ashamed. That is the person I want to be. In regions of my life that fight me into backing away from being confident and secure, I will make an intentional effort to let God renew those areas so I can use my gifts boldly. For those who have been labeled as introverted; I would rather choose to encourage them to walk out of fear and seek to establish God's vision of their identity for their lives.

I understand the intention behind personality profiles, and I am not judging those who use them. What I have found in my life is that those labels have the ability to limit the powerful potential that God has for mankind. Labeling can also cause people to eventually take on the traits and fabricated actions that the label spoken over them requires. I personally was labeled in tests as being introverted, and felt myself continually drifting towards it, because of the fears that I battled. But it took me quite a bit of time to realize this. Each day, the Lord has been teaching me how to be confident in who I am and to even receive strength out of being bold as I step out of my comfort zones. People who are labeled introverts many times are those who could be using their voice to a greater degree but haven't because of fear.

Uncovering the Problem Behind the Scenes

Yet as deviating as many psychological teachings can be, people like Carl Jung actually had some sense in his findings. He recognized the existence of an evil entity beyond the five physical senses that sought to manifest in the physical realm and bond itself to people's lives throughout the generations. The problem is, he never received the truth to discern how to deal with the voices he heard and the evil impressions he received, which were from an evil kingdom that sought to steal, kill, and destroy him. He also was not able to remedy the evil "karma" that he observed being passed down from parents to their children -- the iniquities of families that passed down legacies of unresolved sin to their children.

This search for truth leads us to answers found in the Word of God. In fact, Romans 7 gives us an opportunity to breathe a fresh sigh of relief, when Paul the apostle transparently admits to the evil that occurred in his life. He unveils a ground breaking revelation to mankind by identifying the evil that operated within him and all of humanity.

Paul's heart was like many of ours; his desire was to do good and honor God. The problem was that he was struggling to consistently accomplish that in his everyday life. In understanding his writing, it does not matter what specific sin he struggled with. What does matter here is *how* he describes sin's inner workings.

For what I do is not the good I want to do . . .
Romans 7:19a (NIV)

That statement in itself should help us feel a little less crazy. *Everyone* has actions they are committing, that in the big picture are not what they want to do. In the case of Paul, he was a man considered to be one of the greatest apostles of all time, admitting that the battle does not just end when you accept Jesus into your life. You *now* have a battle on your hands. Before we accepted Christ into our lives, there was no battle. We were lost and destined for defeat. Once we entered into God's Kingdom, we received a new armor and a redeemed battle plan for life. This battle is one that God has given us weapons to win, because Christ has won. But it is still a battle we are in nonetheless.

Paul's heart-felt articulation continues . . .

> . . . *the evil I do not want to do – this I keep on doing.*
> **Romans 7:19b (NIV)**

Is Paul saying that he has two personalities? Or is he bringing to the surface an understanding of two kingdoms within us that are at war in the spirit?

Writing in a methodical manner to the Romans and to us today, Paul wrote about the work of the Holy Spirit that seeks to become more a part of our life as we submit to God and His Word. Yet there is also a place called the flesh, the nature of sin and satan's kingdom where the body of sin resides, that desires to manifest deception in our life. In addition, there is an entire evil spirit realm that seeks to perpetuate this work of sin in mankind's life. It is this arena that Paul says keeps kicking up when he fails to do good.

In previous verses, Paul explains that in his flesh, there is nothing good that lives there.[6] Unfortunately, most of Christianity is confused about the meaning of this word flesh, mainly because it has multiple meanings. The Greek word translated *flesh* can refer to the substance of the body, mankind, the human body, the outward appearance, doing things in our *fleshly* strength and many others meanings.

For the purposes of studying this passage and understanding sin, the flesh in this portion of Scripture speaks of *the spiritual nature of satan's kingdom that God did not originally create us with.* It is a nature that opposes God and seeks to find its way to life apart from God and His Holy Spirit.

God did not originally create you with the flesh or with sin. His identity for you involves being victorious over sin and walking in the Spirit, free from fear in your life. Yet because of wrong choices affect us and our generations, sin's nature has entered the lives of humanity. As a result, we end up being born with this nature; in desperate need for Christ to lead us into victory and into a life of walking free in the Spirit.

The flesh is the seat of sin; where the nature of satan's kingdom wars against your spirit and renewed mind to manifest destruction in your life. It is the place where this living, breathing being of sin lies. It is the seat of iniquity, which many times as shown in Scripture as areas of sin that are inherited in families. Do you ever notice that many of the struggles your parents had are some of the same exact battles, that you hate, yet still encounter yourself? Have you noticed that many of those ungodly desires and thoughts were never taught to you—yet you found that your parents struggled with the same inward battles? This is the work of iniquity that David said he was born into.[7] And when you and I come into agreement with sins ways, we execute its influence as it manifests through us.

In this passage, Paul makes a distinction of a presence within him that is not a part of God's original design, yet has joined him and has committed the action of sin through him.

Now if I do what I do not want to do, it is no longer I who do it, but it is sin living in me that does it.

Romans 7:20 (NIV)

Here we have Paul the Apostle, whose spiritual resume is remarkable, admitting to an indwelling presence of sin within him. He clearly states that when he's doing something he does not want to; *it is not him doing it*. There is another presence that is doing it through him. This body of sin desires desperately to work in his life, and when he is not doing the good he wants to, sin takes opportunity to manifest.

Is Paul releasing himself of responsibility? Certainly not. He was revealing that our *agreement* with the enemy's devices partners with the body of sin through us to manifest sin in this world. Paul's admonition to us is to continually fight it and destroy that evil kingdom through the delivering power of Jesus Christ and a renewed walk.

When Paul revealed the kingdom of darkness and sin, he used many opportunities to give us a greater glimpse into its schemes. In addition, he used just about every phrase possible to give us the understanding of how important it is to wage war against this body of sin and live from the victory found in Christ Jesus. His descriptions are numerous in Romans alone:

- Crucify it (Romans 6:6)
- Destroy it (Romans 6:6)
- Reckon yourself dead to it (Romans 6:11)
- Do not let it reign (Romans 6:12)
- Let not your members yield to it (Romans 6:13)
- Do not allow it to have dominion over you (Romans 6:14)
- Do not serve it (Romans 6:15-20)

The Enemy and Sin

This body of sin seeks to find any way to manifest in our life, and satan's kingdom is the executor of sin's work in our life. So exactly how does the enemy have access to us? The biggest door point is sin. For example, because fear is sin, when we come into continual agreement with it, a spirit of fear brings persistent torment and bondage into our life. That is why repentance is critical to accomplish true deliverance and victory in spiritual warfare. Without it, we end up shadow boxing in warfare towards anything we can think of without much success.

In addition, what this revelation accomplishes is that it gives us the answer to the question: *why do we do the things we do not want to do.* It also helps us identify where these thoughts, impressions, and impulses to do evil come from. They do not come from us, but from something that we have come into agreement with that has joined us. Most of all, this understanding of sin and satan's kingdom gives believers the opportunity with spiritual eyes to separate the part of them that is not *them.* Fear is not you and does not have to be a part of your life anymore. This also reemphasizes the truth that we need to separate *from,* not integrate *with* sin in our lives.

What is Sin?

In understanding the word *sin*, doing some word studies can prove to be helpful and effective. Many times sin is taught only as meaning "to miss the mark". Yet that is the definition of the *verb* of sin, which speaks of us missing the *glory* of God, our original intended place of fellowship.[8] The word *sin* used in Romans 7:20 is a noun. It speaks of a body and kingdom of sin dwelling within us that the enemy seeks to use in order to manifest destruction and torment in our world. For the most part, the enemy cannot just manifest out of thin air; they need human beings to work through.

Jesus was not born with sin, because He needed to be the perfect sacrifice. Yet He was tempted in all ways but did not commit sin. With that in mind, Christ's purity gave no place for the devil and evil spirits to bring torment or oppression into his life. That is why Jesus could confidently say the ruler of this world had nothing in Him. [9] Because we are born with sin and have committed sin, we have to deal with this flesh, the residing place of sin and the nature of satan's kingdom.

Do not fear, but in fact, take a deep breath and relax. *Fear is not you*. It is of sin and of the devil. The truth is, fear may be working *in* you, but it is not *you*, and it needs to be removed. This does not excuse us from personal responsibility that comes when we sin, but it releases us from thinking that we are crazy and insane. It also helps us to stay away from condemnation every time we fall into fearful patterns, knowing that fear is not a part of our nature in Christ.

This can be difficult in our daily application, because when fear speaks, it sounds like its coming from our own thoughts. In fact, the voice sounds like our own voice. The thoughts of fear usually mask themselves by coming through in first person. Yet through this teaching, you can understand that sin is not you. Fear is not you. It is from another kingdom and as a believer, you have the power through Jesus Christ to execute death to the flesh and live in the power of God over fear.

You are not a lunatic and you are not alone. Millions of believers like you have the same struggle that Paul did, and there is certainly a way out as we will discuss further.

See Yourself Set Apart From Sin

For many, there is a tendency to see themselves and others as being *one* with sin. As shown in the illustration below, they view themselves and others through the lens and filter of past committed sins or currently "discerned" sins. In the case of fear, when it manifests itself in your body through anxiety, stress, worry, or panic, you assume that the problem is *you*. But if you look at fear through the lens of Romans 7, you will start to see that fear is *not you*. Although working *in* you, fear is not you. This can be tricky because the symptoms of fear are manifesting in your physical body through rapid pulse, hot flashes, or sweating.

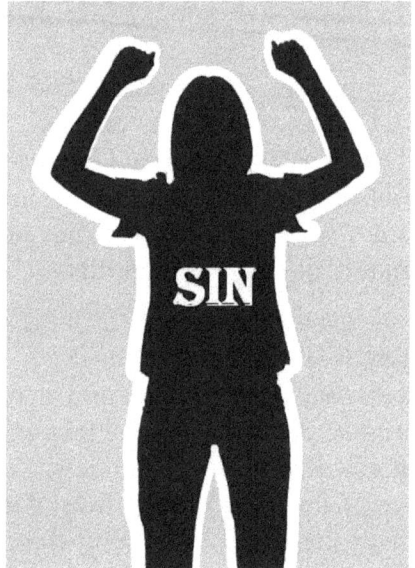

For too many, when fear strikes at their door, it comes as a strong thought along with feelings of panic, anxiety or terror. The deception takes place when fear portrays itself as a thought that came from your own identity and thought process. Although sometimes this is true, we need to get to the root of where the bondage of fear truly comes from.

Through spirit, mind, body connections that we will discuss later, fear gets you to believe that the symptoms of torment that you are sensing are a result of your lousy ability to "keep it together." Yet a major breakthrough will come when you first recognize that sin is *not you*. Fear is sin, and it is not you. It is not a part of your divine identity in Christ Jesus.

God did not create mankind with sin. What has happened is that sin has *joined* man. It has been passed through the generations and is given life when we agree with the thoughts of the enemy. God does not have a plan for fear to be a part of our spiritual DNA. He does not call us to live in fear, but to be free, bold, confident, secure, and loved. As we understand this revelation, we will begin to see ourselves separated from sin, which can help lead us into sanctification (meaning "to be set apart" or separated from).

When we understand that fear is not from God's Kingdom but of sin and the enemy, it helps to create a sense of separation in our thinking and living. With this understanding, we can now separate it from what God sees us to become, while repenting and turning away from fear's devices. This visual is the process of continually being set apart from sin. But we cannot be set apart from fear until we realize that those areas that fear has a lock on are areas of sin that we need to separate *from*. This also helps us to view ourselves through God's eyes, as shown in the picture above.

This revelation has taught me to obtain a much higher edge on fear's tactics. It has also helped me to win battles over all kinds of bondage. In addition, learning to separate the sin from the person will help us to forgive, because of the realization that it was not the person that hurt us, but the sin and the enemy within them that came against us. This understanding can open the door for freedom to come in tidal waves.

This revelation has led me to get on my knees in repentance to a loving Father and say, "Lord, I've given in to something that is not of you. I first of all ask you to forgive me for thinking you were involved in making me fearful at all. You have actually commanded me in Your Word *not* to fear, but to trust You. I have not trusted You in some areas of my life and I need to change this. Father, forgive me for letting fear be my voice instead of You. I repent for giving into fear's devices and I renounce fear in every way. From my heart, I give You permission to fill with your love and power those areas that have been polluted with fear. I receive your grace to live in victory, and I ask you to fill me with a greater understanding of my identity apart from fear."

[1] Romans 14:23 – "for whatsoever *is* not of faith is sin."

[2] The Aryan Christ: The Secret Life of Carl Jung by Richard Noll page xv © 1997 Published by Random House, Inc. in New York and Toronto (Note: the author Richard Noll is a clinical psychologist, and says himself that he is not a Christian or a Jew. He is simply writing from a historical perspective.)

[3] The Aryan Christ: The Secret Life of Carl Jung by Richard Noll page xv © 1997 Published by Random House, Inc. in New York and Toronto

[4] http://en.wikipedia.org/wiki/Carl_Jung

[5] The Aryan Christ: The Secret Life of Carl Jung by Richard Noll page 41 © 1997 Published by Random House, Inc. in New York and Toronto

[6] Romans 7:18

[7] Psalms 51:5 – "Behold, I was shapen in iniquity; and in sin did my mother conceive me.

[8] Romans 3:23

[9] John 14:30

Chapter 10

When Fear Began In This World

I heard thy voice in the garden, and I was afraid . . .
Genesis 3:10

In order to understand the historical operation of fear, let us take a journey to the beginning of Scripture and see its earliest recorded manifestation. The onslaught of fear began on this earth much earlier than most people tend to realize — at the first sight of sin's entrance.

We start off with creation by getting God's view of his handiwork.

And God said, Let us make man in our image, after our likeness: and let them have dominion over the fish of the sea, and over the fowl of the air, and over the cattle, and over all the earth, and over every creeping thing that creepeth upon the earth. So God created man in his own image, in the image of God created he him; male and female created he them. And God blessed them, and God said unto them, Be fruitful, and multiply, and replenish the earth, and subdue it: and have dominion over the fish of the sea, and over the fowl of the air, and over every living thing that moveth upon the earth.
Genesis 1:26-28

To gain a clearer picture, it is imperative to see that when God initiated the creation of mankind, He spoke an *identity* and a *purpose* to His creation. God's specific words were to create man in the image of the Godhead. The word "image" means a shadow, phantom or resemblance. In this case the word is also translated with the English word statue, which means "a copy or image." This term communicates the *representation of the real thing*.

Our identity is found through the eyes of our Creator, who bestowed an image of His qualities into the male and female creation. Through that identity, God gave mankind an original purpose: to have dominion over creation, take care of the earth and multiply the population. His creation was perfect and His purposes were eternal. The satisfaction of God is revealed in the word that went forth to describe it.

And God saw every thing that he had made, and, behold, <u>it was very good.</u>
And the evening and the morning were the sixth day.
Genesis 1:31

It is amazing that God did not just say *good*, because for most, hearing the Creator speak of something as *good* would communicate volumes of satisfaction. But God took it another step. He called His creation *very good*. In the beginning, before the effects of satan and his kingdom were able to manifest through sin, the work of creation was *very good*. That is man's original intended design. Ever since man fell into the trappings of sin, God worked His plan to bring eternal redemption to mankind and to lead us back to our rightful place of identity and purpose.

The Original Design

Before the fall came, the purposes of God were laid out to his creation. He gave Adam, a son of God[1], a job description which was very clear.

And the LORD God took the man, and put him into the garden of Eden to dress it and to keep it. And the LORD God commanded the man, saying, Of every tree of the garden thou mayest freely eat: But of the tree of the knowledge of good and evil, thou shalt not eat of it: for in the day that thou eatest thereof thou shalt surely die.
Genesis 2:15-17

God put Adam in the garden to serve over, watch and keep (or guard) creation. In the earliest stages of creation, God gave man a role to play as guardian and keeper for the family. The Lord gave him a charge: to follow a simple command of obedience. This command would serve to keep the works of an evil enemy that was lurking in the second heavens out of the garden and off the planet. It was a simple command. Even though people many times hate boundaries and orders, even in a perfect community, there was *still* one command. Yet in this world, there was only one: *do not eat of the tree of the knowledge of good and evil.*

Satan's Plan of Deception

Satan, an ex-arch angel and defiant created being was banished from God's heaven into what many believe to be the second heaven because of his rebellion. He was bound there with no ability of expression, except through agreement from mankind. With that in mind, satan sought to bring confusion and deceit to the one whom Adam was chosen to cover, protect and keep: Eve. Satan launched his attack by channeling himself through one of the more cunning animals of creation, the serpent, and he presented himself to Eve.

Now the serpent was more subtil than any beast of the field which the LORD God had made. And he said unto the woman, Yea, hath God said, Ye shall not eat of every tree of the garden? And the woman said unto the serpent, We may eat of the fruit of the trees of the garden: But of the fruit of the tree which is in the midst of the garden, God hath said, Ye shall not eat of it, neither shall ye touch it, lest ye die.

Genesis 3:1-8

The accuser comes in to question if Eve even knows the command that God gave to Adam. If he could find any vulnerability by way of ignorance, lack of knowledge, doubt or confusion, he was going to take it. Eve's response is interesting, because she adds a phrase to the command that was not originally there. She says that they were not allowed to eat of the tree *or touch it.* Yet God did not say they couldn't touch it, which tells us that Adam probably did not clearly communicate and pass on the command correctly to Eve.

With that potential vulnerability, satan tempts Eve to doubt that God's word is true:

And the serpent said unto the woman, Ye shall not surely die: For God doth know that in the day ye eat thereof, then your eyes shall be opened, and ye shall be as gods, knowing good and evil.

Genesis 3:4-5

Satan presents doubt to Eve by saying that God is really holding out on them and does not have their best interests at heart. He deceives her and leads her to believe that God is worried they will be able to know good and evil and in the process, become more like a god or even like the Living God. With this evil agreement, sin was able to take root and with it, a kingdom of wickedness was able to have access to this earthly realm.

Adam's Role

And when the woman saw that the tree was good for food, and that it was pleasant to the eyes, and a tree to be desired to make one wise, she took of the fruit thereof, and did eat, and gave also unto her husband with her; and he did eat.

Genesis 3:6

Notice that the pleasantry of the fruit and the lure to gain wisdom against the ways of God drew Eve in to fall under the temptation, which gave room for sin to be birthed. Yet there is something very critical to make mention of here in this passage. *Adam is standing right there with her.* Many think that Adam showed up randomly and ignorantly ate the fruit that Eve gave to him. Yet through this whole temptation, he was there and let this whole process occur. Not only did Adam fail to stop this evil encounter, he ate of the fruit himself. Even though he had every opportunity as the keeper of the garden to stop this mess and keep the workings of satan out of Eden, he chose to stand by and eat the fruit.

Adam knew exactly what was happening. In fact Paul says in 1 Timothy 2:14 that "Adam was not deceived, but the woman being deceived was in the transgression." Adam could have put a halt to this whole deception through his leadership, but instead he let it occur and also participated. Meanwhile satan took advantage.

Being Uncovered

Much of fear's tactics have had greater room to operate because people have not been properly covered, loved and instructed — especially by men in their lives. God has given men a unique role to guard, protect and love in a way that is unique to them. The problem is that today, millions of people, both men and women, have broken hearts because they have not been shown the love and protection from men; whether it be a husband, father or male authority figure.

God gave one commandment to Adam: do *not* eat of the tree. Adam's responsibility was to convey that command properly to Eve and then guard against it being disobeyed or compromised. Instead, he allowed Eve to be deceived and went along for the ride. In addition to that, later in this passage Adam begins to blame Eve for the whole thing, when in reality He had shrugged off his God given responsibility.[2]

This is not meant to bring condemnation or unnecessary judgment upon men. It is a call for the church to proactively minister to the broken hearts of men and women. In addition, we must address the need for men to be spiritually fathered into becoming godly leaders, who will impart the love of Father God to their families and their world. This call to guard and keep will bring healing to our land and will lay a new foundation of love for generations to come.

The Drastic Change

And the eyes of them both were opened, and they knew that they were naked; and they sewed fig leaves together, and made themselves aprons.
Genesis 3:7

Instantly, the power of sin and torment entered the lives of Adam and Eve. Immediately their perception changed while uncleanness, unlovingness, shame and fear entered in to make their nakedness feel forbidden. Their attempts to rectify the situation were futile as they quickly covered themselves and ran in fear to hide from the voice and presence of their Lord.

And they heard the voice of the LORD God walking in the garden in the cool of the day: and Adam and his wife hid themselves from the presence of the LORD God amongst the trees of the garden.

Genesis 3:8

While hiding, they could hear the voice of God who was seeking to walk with them in the cool of the day. Yet their sin and torment was now keeping them from being able to walk in God's glory and receive His love and intimacy freely. There had been a time when they did not need to even cover themselves. The animals all had coverings of skin, fur, feathers or scales, but Adam and Eve were covered by the glory of God! Yet all that was lost.

As God approached these two, He knew in His omniscience that Adam and Eve sinned, yet in His mercy He still sought them out to commune with them. Sadly, His love and compassion could not be received by His creation, because they were filled with fear.

Adam Where Are You?

Then the Lord God called to Adam and said to him, "Where are you?"
Genesis 3:9 (NKJV)

Did God know that Adam and Eve sinned? Of course He did. Yet He still called out to them and sought after them to come out and talk with Him. God surely could have come out and vaporized Adam and Eve instantly for disobeying the *one* command that He gave them. Instead, He called out for His two most precious creations on the planet for intimacy. Interestingly enough, God has been doing that with mankind ever since. Fear along with shame, guilt, lies and feelings of unlovingness kept Adam and Eve from responding freely to God's call for intimacy.

Who Told You That?

And he said, I heard thy voice in the garden, and I was afraid, because I was naked; and I hid myself.

Genesis 3:10

Fear is now in operation and Adam, not having experience in discerning good and evil is now *one* with fear. He says, "I *was* afraid." He was in essence saying, "I am fear." He didn't realize that fear was not a part of his original spiritual DNA. What took place is that through thought, fear joined Adam and made him think those thoughts and feelings of anxiety were *him*. Quite a deception!

> *And He said, "Who told you that you were naked?"*
> **Genesis 3:11a (NKJV)**

The emphasis on the word *who* is very crucial here, because it gives us insight into fear and the source of fearful thoughts and impressions. Thoughts do not just enter from somewhere in outer space. *They come from a source.* They either come from God, your own system of thoughts that you've gathered, or from satan's kingdom. In this case, this fear was not a part of Adam's life. He lived a life in Eden without fear. This thought certainly did not come from God, because He does not operate in fear, nor is fear a part of His character.

The *who* that told Adam to be afraid is the *who* that I want to firmly address in the next chapters. The *who* is your enemy that seeks to paralyze you with fear and keep you from ministering as God's servant in boldness, confidence and love. This enemy is a *spirit of fear* that has been in operation ever since Adam and Eve, and desires to manifest itself in our world through any way possible, to keep humanity in a prison of ongoing torment.

There is a way of freedom that reveals how minuscule in comparison the enemy is to the presence and power of Almighty God.

---

[1] The Genealogy of Jesus Christ - Luke 3:38 (KJV) . . . Which was *the son* of Enos, which was *the son* of Seth, which was *the son* of Adam, which was *the son* of God.

[2] In the Old Testament Scriptures of the law, God showed His people the principle of a man covering his wife or a father covering his unmarried daughter. In those instructions, God stated that a man could step in and nullify an agreement made by his wife if he is not in

agreement or he sees potential danger (Numbers 30). This was established by God as a way for men to stand as a godly priest and leader in the home.

SECTION III

Victory Over Fear

Chapter 11

Spiritual Bondage Must Be
Dealt With Spiritually

For God hath not given us the spirit of fear . . .
2 Timothy 1:7

We now arrive at a crucial place of understanding for true victory to be found over this enemy called fear. *Fear is a spirit, and because it is a spirit, it operates on a spiritual level and must be dealt with spiritually.* It can very difficult to combat fear simply with natural man's tools and abilities. The reason I say this is because fear operates above the five physical senses through an unseen reality. It is from this unseen realm that fear maneuvers to bring destruction and torment on anyone it can. This is not meant to invoke more fear, but to bring a greater awareness of fear's operations.

More than Just an Emotion

Fear is not simply a psychological defect or just an emotion. It is also not a random chaotic assembly of floating thoughts that accidentally landed into our brain. The Bible calls fear a *spirit*[1], which helps us for a number of reasons.

The Scriptures give us "snap shot" glimpses into the spirit realm that help us see where our battles lie and who our enemy truly is. There is a spiritual nature to fear that operates from satan's kingdom to create torment and bring about systems of thought and action that are contrary to God's ways. Fear perpetuates the work of sin within mankind because its nature *is* sin. Throughout the Scriptures, we can see that sin, darkness and the works of satan are *spiritual* in nature, yet they want to manifest in our physical world.

When a person is bound with fear in any way, they often have a hard time simply thinking and acting differently by their own will and ability. Many under the bondage of fear have a "back-seat" driver that seems to continually nag them with thoughts and impressions without relief. This is the *spirit of fear* that needs to be reckoned with.

A person who is fighting fear of any kind needs to come to the realization that the situation is *first a spiritual one*. The church today has to a great extent lost the truth that our major struggles in life have roots in arenas that are spiritual. Sin is a *spiritual* issue; otherwise we would not need the spiritual weapons of warfare that God gave us to fight the enemy.

Paul reminds us that we wrestle *not* against flesh and blood and our mode of battle is not simply in the physical dimension[2]. Because so many have forgotten this, they have become blind to the heavenly war that is going on.

The victory has been won by Jesus Christ and our responsibility, when we come into a relationship with God through Christ, is to appropriate that victory by faith in our lives daily. If you are a believer, the difference between you and the unbeliever is that *you* have the weapons necessary to defeat your enemy. Yet sadly enough, too many have become ignorant of satan's devices and are serving fear's every signal. Because of this, they fail to walk in the authority and freedom Jesus paid for. It is now time to use the weapons that are at our disposal to fight and overcome. Natural human means alone will not defeat fear's operations.

You Are a Spirit Who Has a Soul and Lives in a Body

In understanding true freedom and spiritual warfare, it is important to first know how God made us and designed us. You *are* a spirit who *has* a soul that *lives* in a body. It is in that sequence. You do not *have* a spirit, you *are* a spirit. The Scriptures teach that when you die, your spirit is what lives on, in either heaven or hell for eternity. Your body is simply the temporary earthen container that you live in during your time here on this planet. Your body's divine design is to be a temple or habitation for the Spirit of God to dwell in. When you die, your body goes back to the dust while your spirit goes to God who gave it and ultimately determines your eternal destiny.[3] Your spirit's destiny will be eternal death in hell unless it is made alive to God through the work of Christ Jesus. (For more information on a relationship with God, see the back appendix.)

When we accept the work of Christ in our lives, it is in our spirit that God places His Holy Spirit to guide us into salvation, healing, sanctification and many other wonderful gifts. We are spiritual beings having an earthly experience; not earthly beings having a spiritual experience.

Our soul is comprised of our mind, thoughts, beliefs, emotions, long term and short term memories and our personality. Our soul is the composition of all the thoughts and beliefs that we value and meditate on. It is a place that must be renewed and submitted to the spirit of God and His ways. A renewed soul will make room for great health and prosperous living to come into our life. In addition, the soul receives the benefits or the consequences of what takes place in the spirit man.

A Revelation of the Spirit Man and Thought Pathways

Many Christians live in the dark ages spiritually because they have not fully recognized the spirit and its activities. They also do not realize the spiritual origin of thoughts and the ramifications they can have on our lives. It is imperative that we recognize *where* thoughts come from and realize that not every thought originates in our own mind. All thoughts do have one certain thing in common: *they come from a source*. A thought does not present itself to us out of thin air as many assume. We can certainly recall thoughts that we have meditated over from our soul. But our spirit acts as a spiritual radio receiver, and is able to receive thoughts and impressions that originate from the Holy Spirit or another spirit.

Through a study of the Scriptures, we can see that the Holy Spirit speaks to our spirit. We cannot see Him with our five physical senses, but through the spirit realm, He can send thoughts and impressions to confirm the Word of God in our life and communicate God's design for us. The Spirit of God also brings revelation, confirmation and witness when we receive truth from God's Word. God wants to release the wonders of His Kingdom into a believer's spirit so that they can receive and deposit the thoughts and ways of the Kingdom here on earth. God's Spirit speaks on a spiritual plane because He *is* spirit. In fact, the Word of God is spirit.[4] When a person communicates with God, they do so through their spirit to speak *to* Him and hear *from* Him. It is an unseen realm from heaven that we learn to connect with by grace through faith.

At the same time, our spiritual enemy is comprised of a kingdom of beings that operate through spiritual means. Satan, evil spirits, principalities, powers and rulers of darkness communicate on a spiritual level. They cannot communicate in the natural unless they have a human being to channel their message through. They are limited to a spiritual realm of the heavenlies for their communication. Their mission is clear and simple: through thoughts, impressions, oppressions, and the power of sin, they seek to bring death, destruction and bondage to all humanity.

So does a spirit of fear have an ability to speak to people on a spiritual level? Absolutely. If you trace the anxiety, worry and overall fears of a civilization, you will find a spirit of fear at the source of what is manifesting in that society. The workings of fear increase as people in droves came into agreement with what it is communicating. These thoughts from a spirit of fear often attack like wildfire and hit with force, but can also move in subtly, masquerading as "concern" or "harmless worry." Over time, this ignorance of fear leads to symptoms of panic and anxiousness.

The trap occurs when people listen to thoughts from fear and act on them as though they came from their own intellect and good judgment. Meanwhile, God's Holy Spirit is wooing us to stay out of fear's traps, to be anxious for nothing, to have no worry in our life and to trust in the Father's goodness, love and protection.

Fear's Connections

For many folks, fear has had an opportunity to speak with greater power because of the brokenness of their heart and spirit. Not being nurtured, loved, or covered properly — virtuous blessings meant to ward off the power of fear are now absent. This can leave a person with tremendous vulnerabilities to fear.

The book of Proverbs gives insightful revelation into how our spirits can be wounded and broken—making us vulnerable to enemy attacks, especially from fear. This spiritual oppression can lead to prisons of anxiety, dysfunctional relationships and even physical infirmities.

He that hath no rule over his own spirit is like a city that is broken down, and without walls.
Proverbs 25:28

A merry heart maketh a cheerful countenance: but by sorrow of the heart the spirit is broken.
Proverbs 15:13

The spirit of a man will sustain his infirmity; but a wounded spirit who can bear?
Proverbs 18:14

A merry heart doeth good like a medicine [cure]: but a broken spirit drieth the bones.
Proverbs 17:22

As you can see, we must pay attention to our spirit, because often times it needs healing from brokenness and wounds. Those areas of vulnerability can open us up to attacks from fear and lead to breakdowns in our health and wholeness. Proverbs 17:22 says that *a broken spirit dries the bones*. Interestingly enough, the bones are the residing location of our body's marrow, the origin of *immune system cells*. The immune system cells are what need to be in full operation for us to live in health. Yet when we have a broken spirit, fear can attack, causing our body's immune system to not work properly at full capacity; thus often making us vulnerable to sicknesses and diseases that our body would normally fight off rather easily.

This is why many times the journey towards healing and wholeness begins from the inside out; a process beginning with letting the Father God heal areas of brokenness in our life. Healing of those broken areas allows us to become strong in spirit so that we can overcome the wiles of the enemy.

Brokenness from Traumas

Fear will often take advantage of *traumas* in the lives of people by reinforcing a certain past dreadful event with constant thoughts and overwhelming impressions of torment. A traumatic event can be anything from a moment of victimization to an automobile accident. Traumas have varying effects on people, depending on individual vulnerability. Fear uses traumatic moments to jump in and bring playback of the event, while keeping the person vulnerable and tormented with thoughts of future dread.

That is why so many who struggle with fear are unable to just stop thinking that way, because there is a spirit tormenting them. To the person who is under fear's torment, those thoughts and impressions seem to come with control and "take over". For those with broken hearts and wounded spirits, fear shouts like a megaphone to drown out any healing voice of love, power and sanity.

Fear's Game Plan In the Soul and Body

When a person is under the continual torment of a spirit of fear, this thought process becomes mapped onto their mind and memory in the soul. When it becomes a part of a person's soul, it has become a regular way of life. A spirit of fear speaks through a spiritual realm and sends thoughts that when accepted, become mapped onto the soul. This is how people can become so deeply programmed to think and live according to the ways of fear, especially in specific areas.

For example, someone who struggles with a fear of the future will eventually become programmed at a soul level to continually think and meditate about being worried and afraid of tomorrow's events. Every time the hard drive of the brain accesses thoughts of tomorrow, fear has programmed the person to continually think of what could happen badly in the future.

Fear's work does not end there. The mind and body are also connected. Because of the constant torment in the spirit and soul, the human body is also receiving the signals of fear's attack. The effects are now taking place on all three levels. Fight or flight in the body is in long term operation and all types of malfunctions are manifesting. The effects over time can be very damaging, even if they occur at minimal, yet constant levels. Over the long haul, because the body is not able to maintain health and immunity, the effects of anxiety, stress and worry are now taking their toll on the person in the form of mental struggles, physical disease and all kinds of ailments.

A Pin-Pointed Attack on Fear's Effects

The good news is, with this understanding, we can start attacking issues of fear in our lives with greater purpose, power and accuracy. It is time that we stop allowing ourselves to be victims of fear's power, but take our rightful place of authority and freedom through Christ Jesus. The backseat driver that has been playing games with God's children needs to be removed and its tactics need to come to an end in our generations.

I am very passionate about this point, because the enemy would love to see a spirit of fear inflict torment on those who desire to do great things for God. He did it to me for years, and I have seen it happen over and over again to those have became ignorant of satan's devices. Satan and his kingdom would love nothing more than to see a spirit of fear bind us from taking any risks and stepping out in faith. He would love to keep us from operating in supernatural power and from knowing firmly who we are as God's children.

That is why I have such zeal to attack fear. It is the very thing that is keeping many from a life of freedom, boldness and empowerment. It tried to trap and destroy me and it failed. Now it is time for recompense as we proclaim the battle cry of freedom!

The Path to Freedom

So how do we begin the path of regaining our sanity and claiming victory in these areas that fear once dominated? How do we begin to walk towards healing in our life? You may be surprised to know this, but there *is* a pathway to victory. God has not left us to fend for ourselves, but has given us tools to repel and vanquish the onslaughts of fear.

Honestly Acknowledge That Fear Has Been Influencing Us

For most of us, we have to simply come to a place of acknowledging that fear has been sneaking into areas of our life and we have listened to its message. We have meditated on fear's thoughts and have obeyed its demands in many ways. For freedom to begin, the excuses and the false justifications need to end. Without condemnation, we must come to a place of being honest before God in recognizing that we have entertained and followed the voice of fear.

With this recognition, it is time we call our constant "concern" what it really is—fear. It is time that our "carefulness" and "nervousness" and "drivenness" be called what it needs to be called—fear rooted. We must be honest with ourselves and God by recognizing that fear is not a part of our design and is *sin*. In that recognition, we approach God from a place of honesty and humility that allows Him to move in our hearts with great power.

Repent for Allowing Fear to Work in Our Life

One of the great gifts that God has given us that satan cannot bypass and work against is *heart-felt repentance*. Repentance involves having a change of mind and turning in a new direction. Satan and his kingdom work through agreement. When we eliminate that agreement through repentance, combined with recognizing our spiritual authority, we make room for God's sanctifying power to deliver us. The power of the cross comes into effect to break the chains of sin and bondage when a believer comes to a place of heartfelt repentance. True repentance occurs when we believe in our heart to obey God and walk in a new direction by His grace.

Some that operate in spiritual warfare fail to understand repentance as a major weapon in deliverance and healing. Too often, many methods will not teach or emphasize repentance from serving fear as a way to become free. You can bind a spirit of fear all you want, but unless you repent from serving it and agreeing with it, you may go right back out the door to serve its promptings again.

This is not a word of condemnation and must be understood with the love of God as a foundation. This is not God beating us on our heads to repent. Repentance simply means breaking our agreement with fear and turning away from what fear has taught us to do. Of course, repentance is only effective when it truly comes from the heart. When we give God our heart, we give him access to make all kinds of renovations in our spirit, soul and body.

Maybe the words of this prayer can be helpful. Don't just read it as a mantra, but make it your own. It can also be extremely profitable if you have someone there with you to pray and agree with you.

Father God, You are a loving heavenly Father who has good gifts for me, Your child. I come before You and acknowledge that I have been listening to fear and have served its commands and promptings. I have not trusted You and Your love for me in the way that I should. I repent for coming into agreement with the fear of _____ and for being led by that fear. I renounce any connections to fears ways. I stand in my authority as a child of God and I tell that fear of _____ to leave my life right now in the name of Jesus Christ. Father, I ask you to fill that place which was once tormented with fear, to be filled with your love.

Spirits of Fear Must Be Removed with Spiritual Authority

I have seen psychosis, anxiety, and even diseases that were spiritually rooted in fear begin to change and heal when the influence of a spirit of fear is removed. Yet this is simply the beginning of what God is doing. The church is coming to a deeper and deeper realization that current trends and methods are falling terribly short of helping people to become free. The simple truth must come to the surface: true *spiritual* changes can only come through *spiritual* steps taking place first.

When ministering to someone dealing with fear of any kind, it is important to lead them (in love) to a place of honest acknowledgement and repentance. When that occurs, speak to those spirits of fear and tell them to remove their hold in the name of Jesus. This does not always happen in two seconds, but it begins a domino effect of personal deliverance from fear.

Countless people have received relief and freedom from torment as a result of the power of God working through the authority of Jesus name. You can partner with someone you trust to minister to you, but you can certainly take authority yourself!

A Testimony of Freedom

One example that comes to mind is when I ministered to a woman during a service where I preached and taught on the issue of fear, rejection and God's love. Towards the end of the service, there was a swell of voices that spoke in honest repentance from people who needed freedom. There is one woman who came forward that I will never forget.

She came to the altar, and a friend of hers motioned to me that she needed help getting rid of some serious fear issues. I walked over to her and asked if she acknowledged fear was working and repented for agreeing with it. I came into joined with her desire to be free and looked into her eyes to speak to that kingdom that was tormenting her. In the spirit I could discern that there was a spirit of fear in the form of terror that had brought relentless torment to her. In fact, I could see it in her eyes. As I told it to leave her, I saw it manifest in her face. Extreme terror and absolute fright came to her expression as I told it to leave in the name of Jesus.

Often when people become free from a spirit of fear, they sense a swell of peace and serene relief come over them. This case was a little different. Immediately a shriek of horror came from her mouth and she fell back on the floor like a brick. With that occurrence, I knew this needed a little bit of attention. With others around in support, I picked her back up.

My next words were said with love, because I wanted to see my sister in Christ free. With authority I said, "You spirits of fear and terror, I command you in the name of Jesus to leave this woman for good and don't ever come back!" As I said this I could see a massive sigh of relief wash over her as color and calmness flushed back to her face. I began to speak the love and peace of God into those areas that had been tormented by fear, and it was obvious that there was a dramatic change.

After this incident I took this woman aside and she immediately expressed a slight bit of embarrassment regarding the outbursts that came out of her mouth. Her words were, "That *was not me!* You have to understand, that was *not* me!" I couldn't help but laugh because she was exactly correct. *It was not her.* It was another kingdom that had been removed. She continued by telling me more of her story.

Through my discussion with this woman, my thoughts about her bondage were confirmed. She expressed to me her walk with God and desire to grow in faith, yet she was greatly tormented by a fear for tomorrow, fear of disease, fear of not being safe and worst of all, a fear that made her afraid of God. Our God of grace and mercy was seen as someone to fear and dread rather than as a Heavenly Father of love and protection. Yet on that night, she was able to get a release of freedom through executing God's simple yet powerful weapons of righteousness. I followed up with her years later and found she was still raving about her continued path of freedom, which spring boarded from that night. Her excitement and passion for God and Kingdom work soared to a higher level.

A New Wave of Freedom

This scenario along with many more mark a wave of freedom that will continue to grow as people walk out of anxiety, timidity, insanity, phobias, fear driven patterns, psychosis and diseases rooted in fear by coming into alignment with God's Word and His power. It will happen when the body of Christ regains their spiritual senses and walks in a discernment that God intended for us to have.

It is time that we take our rightful place of authority and stand against the strategies of fear. Stand up to it. Fight it. Don't wait for a minister to lay hands on you. Don't wait for a mystical experience to come. Right now, come before your Heavenly Father who loves you and sent His only begotten Son to die so you could have power over fear. If you have not believed that Christ died for your sins, you can receive Him today and allow His cleansing work to give you a new life. As a believer, bow your heart before a loving Father and ask for His Spirit to bring life and power. Speak to that fear and tell it to leave in the name of Jesus! Don't wait for someone else to deliver you. Take your rightful place of authority against fear. God has given you everything you need to stand up in authority against it.

This freedom will be received more and more as God's gift of boldness rises up in us to fight against fear. Yet the biggest weapon against the terrors of fear is the greatest of all – love. With God's love extended to you and through you, victory can be found and rest can be maintained. Deliverance and freedom have a shaky foundation if they are not founded on the love of God. The next chapter will focus on the perfecting work that love needs to have in all our lives. This may be the most important chapter that you read in this book.

---

[1] 2 Timothy 1:7

[2] Ephesians 6:12 and 2 Corinthians 10:4

[3] Ecclesiastes 12:7 - "Then shall the dust return to the earth as it was: and the spirit shall return unto God who gave it."

[4] John 6:63 (NKJV) - *It is the Spirit who gives life; the flesh profits nothing. The words that I speak to you are spirit, and they are life.*

Chapter 12

The Abba Revelation: Perfected In Daddy's Love

. . . he who fears has not been made perfect in love.
1 John 4:18 (NKJV)

This revelation has been one of the most powerful explosions of truth I have ever received in my life. It has touched lives dramatically in many ways. It has swept the nation and will continue to reach the corners of the world. This revelation is making way for a renewal and a revolution in this world like never before. It has to do with a heart-felt understanding of the love of God through experiencing His love as our Father.

Covered by Abba's Love

When we have made the decision to wage war against the satan's devices, there is a covering that must be experienced, which builds a fortress of strength within us that cannot be penetrated. This involves knowing and relying on the love of Father God in our lives. Yet it is not enough to simply have a head-knowledge of Father God's love. It must arrive by our hearts being touched in a personal experience. If it does not occur through encounter, then it just becomes something to think about. What we need is for His love to consume our entire being and lead us into transformation.

Understanding God's deep love for us begins with receiving His love as our Heavenly Father. Even deeper than that is the intimacy we can have with God as "Abba." The word "Abba" is a Greek word used three times in the New Testament as a way for believers to reference our God in a very intimate way. It is the most intimate name we could ever use to call upon Him. In English, it means, "Daddy." The title "Father" is the more formal term to use, as in when we pray, "Our Father." But "Daddy" or "Papa" speaks of an intimate expression of love, comfort, covering and protection that cannot be matched by any other relationship. The great news is that it is a privileged word that God has given to us as believers to call Him.

Abba Gives Strength to Jesus

One of the uses of this word *Abba* is found in the gospel of Mark 14, where Jesus is in the garden at His hour of greatest need:

And he went forward a little, and fell on the ground, and prayed that, if it were possible, the hour might pass from him. And he said, <u>Abba, Father,</u> all things are possible unto thee; take away this cup from me: nevertheless not what I will, but what thou wilt. (emphasis mine)

Mark 14:35-36

I cannot emphasize this enough: *If Jesus Christ needed to be able to call upon His Daddy in His greatest time of trial, then each and every one of us as God's children must recognize our need to have an Abba relationship with God.* In that moment of tremendous desperation, Jesus called out to His Daddy to help Him through His most trying experience. Because He had a solid relationship with His Father, Jesus was able to draw the strength He needed to submit and remain faithful to the redemptive plan that He was sent to fulfill.

With this revelation of love from *Abba*, we will realize in our hearts that Daddy has good plans for us that He will empower us to carry out. His divine plan for us is backed with unending love and goodness that can equip us to follow our divine destiny with confidence.

An *Abba* relationship communicates daily to us that Daddy has our back, no matter what circumstances approach our horizons. With this powerful revelation, we can experience more of his love, to the degree where fear has no opportunity to invade. Fear loses its edge when we simply know in the depths of our hearts that we are loved, covered, and safe.

Fear Attacks Where Love is Absent

For so many, a broken heart has led to a broken spirit, resulting in a vulnerability to fear's attacks, along with a distorted of understanding of true love. For men, it becomes an endless cycle of not feeling good enough while wondering if anyone has their back. For women, it is the constant sensation that they are not covered and safe.

When we identify the areas where fear is attacking the most, we are also locating the area of our life that needs to be perfected in love. This connection is often present with fear related issues. The brokenness of the spirit has become like a city broken down and without walls, making room for invaders to attack. The armies of fear that those walls were meant to protect you from are now taking advantage of your wounds and hurts.

For so many hurting souls, the love of Father God is so desperately needed to bring a true deliverance and explosive freedom from fear. The vast majority of people do not even know how to begin to understand the love of Daddy God. Of course this mainly comes out of the fact that they were not properly shown that representation in their own parents. The tenderness, love, and approval was not available in their father. The sensitivity, nurturing, and peace from their mother was absent or dysfunctional at best. Traumas, victimizations, and failures all contribute to this vulnerability to fear as well.

I am certainly not uncovering this to place blame and judgment on parents, families or leaders. This is simply a process of allowing the Holy Spirit to reveal areas where we have become vulnerable to fear. Let me also make this very clear: this message is not intended for us to introspectively attempt to dig up every possible shred of dirt we can think of. Unveiling issues that need healing and restoration is the job of the Holy Spirit, who brings illumination as we receive truth. My encouragement is to allow the Spirit of God to lovingly walk you through these issues. His guidance and comfort will guide you through your road to recovery.

Forgiveness Unlocks a Greater Level of Freedom

The mission of fear was clearly intended to keep you locked into living in rejection, torment and bitterness. As we reveal these truths of freedom, forgiveness is going to be an integral component to the healing to the broken heart. Forgiving and releasing those who wounded you will be a foundational step that will unlock more deliverance for you from your past. The love of God ought to lead us to repent for areas where offense, bitterness, anger and resentment have clogged up our ability to walk free from rejection and fear. In fact, Jesus taught that the unforgiving servant was handed over to the *tormentors* because of his unwillingness to forgive others[1].

Forgiveness has such a magnificent power to bring us victory and it is a major theme of what the cross is all about. Allow God even right now to reveal people that you need to forgive, who were used to open the door of rejection and fear into your life; those who should have loved you and cherished you, but instead wounded you. As you walk towards forgiving them, the love of God will be able to enter in greater measure, giving you expanded power over fear and rejection. Forgiving and releasing those who victimized you will help you to stop this rejection from repeating itself in your life. This is also a strong step towards your new life in love.

A New Walk and a New View

Your wounds created an area of brokenness where the enemy attacked, and it allowed a misunderstanding to develop in your thinking of what God looks like to you. Many people told you to simply "get over it," but you never could. You went to counselor after counselor to no avail. Maybe you have even tried doctors or alternative methods. *Yet through it all, you kept hitting a wall, because God needed to heal your broken heart.*

God wanted you to be protected and covered in His love. His design was for you to see His love through those He put in your life. Their failures were not a part of His design, and He wants to heal you and bring freedom into your life. Look at what God said in Ezekiel.

And I will give them one heart, and I will put a new spirit within you; and I will take the stony heart out of their flesh, and will give them an heart of flesh:
Ezekiel 11:19

As a part of this healing process, you need to let your Daddy in heaven heal your brokenness. For many, the phrase *Daddy* in reference to God does not compute in their mind and this is a sign that your heart has been broken in this area. For me, I had a hard time with this concept, because I was always shown that God is a very holy God who cannot be approached in "childish ways." This kept me from knowing that I could jump into His arms and receive His embrace of love and grace. Yet things began to change when I allowed the *Abba* revelation to become a part of my life.

It took a moment of personal experience for that love to begin permeating my heart. A friend that God placed in my life stood in the gap one day and ministered a word of the father's love over me, and it was like God the Father was standing in the room speaking words of affirmation and destiny over me! In addition, this man's wife caringly spoke words of the mother's love, revealing the nurture and tenderness of God that I was not confident in. They were not my parents, but they stood in the gap in that moment as my brother and sister in Christ to minister to those broken areas with love. It began to tear down walls of confusion, fear and rejection that I did not even know existed. This is around the same time that God gave me a revelation of Romans 8:15, which I will share later in this chapter. From that time of *Abba* revelation, I have been on a daily journey of diving into Daddy's love and walking with that love to every destination that He sends me to minister.

Stepping Out Towards Love

The Bible says that perfect love casts out fear. The very presence of true love gives fear an eviction notice. Yet someone who is bound by fear will have a very difficult time giving and receiving love. It is almost impossible to love when you are locked in by fear. At best, you can merely go through the motions, which does not bring the inner fulfillment that comes when you truly give and receive love. You end up feeling trapped. Most who struggle through this may be able to put on a front and survive through the day, but internally they are paralyzed by fear's grip. This is why fear needs to leave so that love can begin to take over your life.

For many of you, you're going to need to face your fears by finding a safe place where you can receive a tangible sense of God's love. This will enhance your deliverance and healing process. I know you may have tried this before, but you probably have not taken a risk for your healing like this in a while. It is time to step out again and trust to see your faith met by God and people that He places in your path.

Let me also encourage you with this word. In your healing process, you're going to have to cut yourself a break and give yourself time to let love heal you. Too many of us want the "drive-through" fix-up, and unfortunately that can add to the problem. Love is not a quick fix. Love is not an addiction rush like many think it to be. Love is not simply something that a minister can slap on you and send you on your way. Love is a divine gift of God, which cannot be simply described; it must be experienced. God is love. He does not just *have* love; He *is* love. When we encounter Him, we ought to be sensing His love in great power. Anything that tries to block you from personally experiencing that pure love is a counterfeit and a deception of satan.

Love says to us, "Chill out and relax. Be at peace, God has the whole universe in control. One day we are going to rule and reign with Him. We might as well start living in that now!" I know it seems easier said than done, but we've allowed the enemy to tell us that this love picture is too good to be true. Yet it's really not. God wants you to be free and He sent His Son to die so you could see how much your Heavenly Father is crazy in love with you.

Fear has caused us to feel stressed out to the point that we as a community are experiencing sicknesses, disorders and diseases in greater numbers. Many of those ailments are rooted in something that God does not want us to carry: fear. We have been so bound up by this spirit of fear that it has affected us on all levels in our life. One of the main things fear wants to keep us from is experiencing that comforting and healing love of God—a love that can heal our past and give us a new future.

My prayer for you is that you will open up to Father God and ask Him to reveal Himself as *Abba* (Daddy) to you. Begin that today by asking Him to show you His love and allow Him to heal the faulty images of love in your life. Let Him heal your broken heart as you cleanse yourself from fear's tactics and immerse yourself in His love. That place once tormented by fear can be filled with Daddy's love.

Abba's Power to Break Rejection and Give You an Identity

For ye have not received the spirit of bondage again to fear; but ye have received the Spirit of adoption, whereby we cry, Abba, Father.
Romans 8:15

God brought me tremendous breakthrough in this passage of Romans as I allowed His love to permeate my life. He showed me that the *spirit of bondage again to fear* that Paul speaks of does not just speak of fear, for in the book of Timothy, he reveals *the spirit of fear.* This passage talks about *a spirit of bondage that makes us a slave to fear.*[2] This is not addressing fear by itself, but more specifically *a spirit of rejection,* the counterfeit to the Spirit of adoption.

Rejection is the counterfeit of God's adoption, because it makes you feel and believe that you do not belong, you are not accepted and you will have to earn any love or approval in your life. It sends you on roller coaster of idolatry as you seek to gain the love and approval of people around you, rather than simply resting in what your Father in heaven says about you.

I bring this subject to the surface because rejection and fear many times go hand in hand and partner with each other to promote dysfunctional lifestyles. The fear of rejection causes people to completely conform their lifestyle and value systems in a way that they never would have normally. Rejection can also lead you to believe and act in ways that end up fulfilling what rejection says to which is, "you are not acceptable".

These ways are contrary to God's ways, because He simply wants us to be content with who He made us to be. His plan is for us to walk without a fear of what anyone thinks of us. God even tells us to kick the dust off our feet from anyone who rejects us and speaks evil of us.

Psalms 118:6 exhorts us by saying, "The LORD *is* on my side; I will not fear: what can man do unto me?" That word, if received with revelation and put into practice in our day to day thinking will change our lives forever. If God truly accepts us, then rejection should have no place in our lives. With this in mind, when walking in freedom from fear, we may also need to come before God and repent for giving into rejection.

A continual, ongoing experience of being at rest in Daddy's love is imperative, because in this experience, we understand that Father God has our back and there is no need to walk in fear. He has given us a spirit of adoption that allows us to cry out "Daddy" and gives us access to being joint heirs with Jesus Christ, not slaves.

Abba Teaches Us to Walk Out of Slavery and Into Sonship

And because ye are sons, God hath sent forth the Spirit of his Son into your hearts, crying, Abba, Father.
Galatians 4:6

This issue of sonship is so critical, because it is the foundation by which fear cannot enter. When I truly live in an on going revelation that I am a son of the Most High God, created in His image to do great works for Him, then fear doesn't stand a chance. Each day my hearts calls on Daddy God for intimacy and strength.

As I have grown in my walk with the Lord, I have learned the value of waking up every morning and giving my heart to Father God. I start off by recognizing that He loves me. I also remind myself that I do not need to do one single thing to earn His love or acceptance during that day. My responsibility is to receive His love and live out of that love throughout the day. When I do this, it changes *everything*.

When we live out of the Father's love, we live as sons and daughters instead of as slaves or servants. Jesus said that He no longer calls His disciples servants, but friends[3], because God is calling His people beyond task oriented living and into personal intimacy with the Father. When I live a task oriented day, I live with a performance mentality that has spiritual "to do" lists attached to it all day long. This usually perpetuates a never ending cycle of serving intended to earn God's love and approval, still feeling unworthy to sit at the table with the Master.

When we live out of intimacy, we value precious time with the Father, knowing that out of that relationship He will reveal His love and character in a way that will dynamically change the way we approach each day. He wants to reveal His love during those times so we can walk without fear and minister *in* love, not *for* love.

It is during those moments of connection that He heals those areas that I am wounded in. Most of all, it is during those times that He will show me a vision of my purpose and destiny, as well as how to pursue it without fear. When I live in intimacy, I can freely sit at the table and receive the greatest meal I could ever taste: the Bread of Life and the Father's heart.

Be Perfected in Love

For most of us, the message these days is not to run around and swing at any devil of fear you can find. There is certainly a level of warfare necessary for every believer. But I have found in addition to deliverance, the message of these last days is for people *to be perfected in the love of Father God.* It is not just a head understanding, for it must be a revelation that comes to our hearts and burns within us. Love is the greatest above *all* things. When we climb to that pinnacle, we find our Father God, who *is* love.

But How Do I Start?

The simple question that is kicking around in many minds is, "How do begin to receive this great love?" Although I wish that I could jump into your room and minister to you, I believe that this *Daddy* revelation is for everyone who will seek for it with all of their heart. Although you can never compress love into steps, allow me to give some thoughts that can help propel you into His arms.

- Open up your heart. This seems very simple, but it is many times a closed or guarded heart that keeps God's love from penetrating. Ask Him to help you in this.

- Remove pride from your life and humble yourself before God to do a healing work. Pride can cause you to harden your heart and it can keep you from allowing yourself to be vulnerable.

- Begin to discover the areas of your life that have not been touched by the Father's love and invite Him in. Recognize that those areas of hurt were not God, but were attacks that the enemy used to bring torment. God wants to come in and intimately bring healing and restoration.

- Begin to address God as your Father[4] and as Dad as best you can. This is not a disrespectful address; it is a privileged relationship that God has given us access to. Earnestly ask Him to give you an experiential revelation of His love. Be patient. He will be faithful to reveal Himself.

- Allow yourself to open up more and more each day for God to love you in those areas where you hurt. Trust Him to lovingly work in your heart. Be open to allow Him to send people and situations your way that become catalysts for healing. Many times when we ask for His love, He will send someone who will love us. Be open to that possibility.

As a close to this chapter, allow me to share with you a letter from a father to his child, which came to me as I was anticipating the birth of my own son. Maybe as you read this letter, you can receive the words as a message to *you*. I invite you to open up your heart and let each word bring a sense of comfort and healing to you life.

My dearly loved child,

*I want you to know that I was so overjoyed when I found out that your mother and I would be birthing you into this world. You have brought a new sense of love into our lives by simply being you. I am so proud to be your father and I want you to know that I will always be proud of you. From my heart I want you to hear these words, **I love you**.*

With that love, I want you to know that I will be here for you to support you, guide you and help you in those times when you need advice or simply need an affirming word, reminding you that "you can make it." I want you to always remember throughout your life that, I've got your back and I will be your biggest cheerleader.

In receiving this love, I want you to learn how to one day love that special person that God brings into your life by watching how your mother and I love each other. As you observe your mother's life, may you see the nurture and admonition of God through the tenderness and care that she faithfully extends to you. I deeply desire for you to see the love of God the Father through me. If I can demonstrate that, then I have been a supernatural manifestation of God's character, because He is love. God designed you for love and I pray that you always live with His love as your highest priority. May you delve deep into the vast seas of His affection for you by knowing that His love is unconditional and free. Although your mom and I will fail you, the love of the Lord has no end and endures without boundaries.

May this love keep you from fear as you realize deep in your heart that God has your life in the palm of His hand. May His sacrificial love remind you to walk free from sin as you daily abide in Christ. We have already released you in dedication to God, but I encourage you to do the same by releasing your heart to Him and giving your life to Him, for He deeply cares for you. He has plans and purposes that are beyond your wildest imaginations. I am so excited for you, because those plans are already being laid out in anticipation of your faithful obedience to God's will.

When you make mistakes, please know that your mother and I are committed to help you through; to be a source of strength as you step out in faith and follow the dreams and visions that God has placed on your heart. I encourage you to dream big, because you are in the hands of a massive God whose ways are beyond comprehension and whose plans are exceedingly abundantly above all you could ask or imagine[5]. The sky is the limit, so be free to reach out for it.

I want you to be secure and free to be you and not anyone else. Let God teach you who you are in Him, and don't let anyone form you into a man-made mold that is not a part of God's precious design for you. Follow the call of God, wherever it leads, knowing that He will lead you at every step and provide for you above and beyond your every need. And while you are living and moving throughout life, know that your Father in Heaven and your Father here on earth are so deeply please to call you, my child.

With all my love,

Your Daddy

For those of you who have not experienced this kind of love, let me first say to you that I am sorry. I am sorry you did not hear those words, *I love you* on a regular basis. I am sorry for those of you who did not hear it at all. I am sorry that you were not shown love, but were made vulnerable to fear.

Yet God's words speak very contrary to those pains. He says with a heart of compassion, *that is not Me. I am not like that. I love you with an everlasting love and I am so pleased to call you My child. Nothing you can ever say or do will make Me love you more or any less. I want you to be content to be My child. I want you to sense my arms wrapping around you, giving you the comfort that says I will never leave you. I am performing good things on your behalf. Would you open your heart to receive them? I love you so much, I sent my Son to die for you, so that you could join the family. I am your Father, and I am asking you to live as my dearly loved child. Will you accept my invitation?*

Let His love heal your broken heart. It will set you free from fear and it will give you a security like you have never had before. It is in this love of the Father that we find our true identity, as we will see in the next chapter.

---

[1] Matthew 18:34

[2] This is how the NIV translates it. Romans 8:15 - *For you did not receive a spirit that makes you a slave again to fear, but you received the Spirit of sonship. And by him we cry, "Abba, Father."*

[3] John 15:15

[4] Matthew 6:9

[5] Ephesians 3:20 (NIV) - *Now to him who is able to do immeasurably more than all we ask or imagine, according to his power that is at work within us . . .*

Chapter 13

Identity Security:
Knowing Who You Are

For we are His workmanship, created in Christ Jesus unto good works,
which God hath before ordained that we should walk in them.
Ephesians 2:10

Whenever there is a significant lack of love in someone's life, there also resides a lack of security. In addition, without our need to be loved being fulfilled, there will be vulnerabilities towards drivenness to prove self worth, value and acceptance. With this dysfunctional pursuit, fear will invade and push a person to pursue an identity outside of God's design. On the other hand, when someone is lovingly secure in their identity, fear doesn't stand a chance.

A Mass Identity Crisis

There exists an identity crisis in the world today where fear has hitchhiked along for the ride. This dilemma has caused confusion in the basic understanding of who we are to *be* and what we were meant to *do* individually. With this vulnerability and confusion often comes a driven pressure to perform, strive and excel at all costs, which in most cases is rooted in rejection and fear. Also, fear drives people who are insecure to build an identity that is not consistent with who they really are. This synthetic persona takes a great deal of extra effort and stress to maintain, because it does not flow naturally.

When a person lacks the understanding of who they really are, fear is constantly at work. Without a confident self-image, folks will live in regular insecurity, worrying if others will discover the mask they are wearing is really a fabrication. That mask, which can manifest in a variety of forms, is intended to keep people at a distance. It also stops people from seeing the real identity underneath which the person is not content and secure with.

In addition, when we are insecure, there is a tendency to create an identity based on what we *do*, rather than simply being settled in who we *are*, and there is a big difference. Having an identity based on who you *are* gives room for failure to occur, knowing that failure is a learning opportunity and not the end of the world. Also, when an identity is secure, there is no need for perfectionism or performance-driven lifestyles.

With that said, performance and perfectionism should not be confused with *excellence*. Excellence should be a desired standard for all believers, and should flow out of our identity in God as His children. Performance, drivenness, striving and perfectionism rule out of a fear of rejection, a fear of failure and a religious spirit. True excellence comes out of an overflow of the Spirit of God working within us, not from our driven efforts to achieve. In fact, contrary to popular opinion, excellence originates out of a passionate heart, not necessarily from extravagant pageantry and elegant appearance.

Without God's presence working through a humble and contrite heart, the work and labor that we attempt will produce mere theatrics. Excellence comes from people who plant continual seeds of submission to God and develop an inner dependence upon His Spirit. This produces Kingdom results that could not even be touched with our own best efforts. When we honestly seek His face for answers and direction, we give God room to operate beyond our best ideas and schemes. Most of all, we are able to accomplish great things when we live as dearly loved children of God, not as wandering paupers searching for an identity.

Performance Ministry

I can remember many times in ministry when I would preach what I considered to be the best and most well thought out messages to a congregation that from my own eyes, should receive and experience drastic results. Yet there were times where I would walk away in utter disappointment, because I was confused as to why God did not arrive to perform over the word I gave in the way I wanted Him to. In addition, there were messages that I gave that I for many reasons fumbled through and did not present in what I considered to be an "A" standard presentation. Little did I know that those "subpar" messages were life changing impartations to those who listened, because I came from a greater level of sincerity and transparency from my heart rather than polished perfectionism. It was during those times that I began to learn how foolish it is for us to pursue false standards of perfection, rather than focusing on coming from the heart in all things.

I learned through experience that my most finely arranged messages were not always my greatest moments of ministry. In God's eyes, the most powerful moments that He could use were times where I came from the simplicity of a humbled heart and dependence upon God to do a significant work.

The body of Christ has become afraid and cowardly. As a result, the church has forgotten its courageous identity and has put on a religious mask that has kept us from full effectiveness. Our biggest breakthrough will unleash when we minister as ourselves, not as someone else. When the people in the church break out of insecurity, the lights will turn on in our cities and the world around will tune in, because they will recognize that we are not just trying to "sell them" something. We will show them that we need the gospel message too and are committed to letting it work in our lives daily.

Excellence communicates that we do the best with what we have, coming from a place of knowing that we do not need to earn God's love or the love and acceptance from those around us. Kingdom excellence comes from transparency that allows God to have the maximum space to move on the hearts of people, and for Him to receive the ultimate glory in the end.

Yet all of this becomes more attainable when we truly understand our *identity*. One day I had the opportunity to hear from a man of God who told me to repeat these words out loud so that I could get this message into my heart. This phrase has performed a piercing work in my life ever since: *Who I am is not _what_ I do, but who I am _is_ what I do.* You change the emphasis, and you change the person's focus and destiny. You are the message. The greater the authenticity of the messenger, the more powerful the message becomes. But the revelation goes even further than that.

Who Do You Say That I Am?

To discover personal security in our identity, the perfect example to observe is Jesus. He showed deep intimacy with His Father, displayed a great deal of security in His identity and was able to pursue a single-minded ministry purpose. In the Gospel of Matthew, we see Him with great wisdom establishing identity values by asking His disciples a very pointed question.

When Jesus came into the region of Caesarea Philippi, He asked His disciples, saying, "Who do men say that I, the Son of Man, am?" So they said, "Some say John the Baptist, some Elijah, and others Jeremiah or one of the prophets."
Matthew 16:13-14 (NKJV)

Like most of Jesus' queries, this was a setup for His teachings to come forth in a very powerful, yet practical way. His question was first to address what outsiders were saying about Him. In their response, the disciples listed out names of great prophets of the past like Elijah, Jeremiah, and a most recent man of the prophetic, John the Baptist.

Now why would people say that Jesus was possibly one of the great prophets? Basically they derived that idea from what they most likely saw Him *do*: speak words with prophetic power. But wasn't Jesus so much more than a prophet when He was here on earth?

Yet even to this day, mankind has such a nasty habit of boxing people in by labeling them based on what they *do*. Labeling places a person into a category of identity. This "pigeon-holing" causes people to be put into a box that can limit their potential. When we see someone who excels well in a certain arena, the automatic reaction many times is to label them into that specific service or work, forgetting that their span of abilities and influence may go way beyond that. Even as children, sometimes those around can put labels upon us. Sadly, we often live the rest of our lives striving to keep up with those labels.

Jesus was not just a prophet; He was a teacher, healer, Savior and many other things. But He did not allow Himself to be limited when people labeled Him with other past prophets. That labeling, especially if it occurs very early on, can limit people because it does not encourage operating outside of the stated purpose of that given title. If we are not careful, we will give little regard for the true identity within people and within us that comes from God, which no man can formulate or manipulate.

He said to them, "But who do you say that I am?"
Matthew 16:15 (NKJV)

Now please understand, Jesus did not need an extra pat on the back when He posed this question. He was opening up the doorway for revelation to come forth to the men that He had invested His life in. Peter, the one who we all can relate to because of his seeming instability at the time, steps forth and astounds Jesus with his response.

Simon Peter answered and said, "You are the Christ, the Son of the living God." Jesus answered and said to him, "Blessed are you, Simon Bar-Jonah, for flesh and blood has not revealed this *to you, but My Father who is in heaven."*
Matthew 16:16-17 (NKJV)

Jesus had a clear understanding of who He was, and out of that identity He flowed with absolute security. Only divine revelation could have shown Peter what this true identity of Jesus was. It is not based on man's pressures or perspectives. With only 3 years of ministry here on earth, Jesus certainly could have fallen victim to the expectations of the crowd or the Pharisees. Their peer pressure could have driven Him into being something that He was *not*, which they certainly tried to impose on Him many times. They even attempted to use Scripture as a way to manipulate Him into the person *they* wanted Him to be. But our Savior and Lord was never moved by those man-made demands. He was confident in who He was and confident in His purpose.

One of the greatest examples of how secure Jesus was is in John 11 when Lazarus, a man that Jesus loved, was sick and heading towards death. Jesus knew this was not going to end tragically, but Lazarus was going to be a display of the glory of God through a miraculous encounter. Yet most people, hearing of the news that a loved one is sick, would change their plans immediately to make sure they rushed to be with the person.

Jesus defies all cultural systems and social structures of politeness by deciding to wait 2 days. Can you imagine a close loved one hearing that you are deathly ill and making up their mind to wait 2 days to even show up or call! Yet Jesus was beyond secure, he was eternally smooth in his security. With that solid confidence, He was able to operate completely under the direction of Father God and raise Lazarus from the dead. It allowed Jesus to be sensitive to divine direction, leading Him to bring healing through an unorthodox set of actions.

Jesus was the Son of the Living God and His sonship was never tainted or distorted. This identity remained intact and secure in Him. Because of that, He was able to clearly maintain His purpose, which was to be *the Christ, the Messiah*; the One who would bring salvation to all mankind. Out of that moment, Jesus was able to impart the importance of *identity security* to Peter.

Who Is Peter?

And I also say to you that you are Peter, and on this rock I will build My church, and the gates of Hades shall not prevail against it. And I will give you the keys of the kingdom of heaven, and whatever you bind on earth will be bound in heaven, and whatever you loose on earth will be loosed in heaven."

Matthew 16:18-19 (NKJV)

Just as Christ's name means "Messiah", Peter's name means "Rock" which would give him a new lens to identify himself. Jesus was communicating that although Peter was struggling and possessed some inconsistencies, he had just received a revelation regarding the identity of his Master. Jesus then quickly transitioned into a prophetic utterance regarding Peter's identity, by speaking to his name and to the future church.

He revealed to Peter in the same way that God often speaks to us—through the lens of what He sees us to *become*, not as we presently *are*. Many times we view our identity through our sins and struggles. Yet God sees us through a lens of what *He* intends for us to become. Upon this revelation of identity, Jesus was building His church; a glorious body that would exemplify the manifestation of God's saving love and power.

Jesus calls Peter a rock, yet at this time, Peter was not exactly what you would call a solid rock. Often he was anything *but* a rock. In fact, much like you and I, he stumbled through finding his way towards understanding the Kingdom. He even struggled to stay loyal to the Savior during His crucifixion, as Jesus predicted and warned. Peter would deny Christ three times, but in this passage of Scripture Jesus is not pointing to Peter's faults, He is pointing to a stable rock of a man who in the prophetic future would operate at a supernatural level of power. I bet when Peter stood before the people on the day of Pentecost and preached with boldness, the exhortation of Jesus here in Matthew 16 came back to memory.

The Power of a Secure Identity

Along with Jesus' words of "identity security" given to Peter came a spiritual authority that would shake the gates of Hell at its hinges. Yet that power and authority would not come through academia or strategic positioning, it would arise out of a security in the personal identity that God gave him. Not only would Peter walk in great power during his generation, but a foundation was being laid in that moment for the church to possess in generations to come. The body of Christ would be a rock with Jesus as her chief cornerstone. The keys of heaven would be handed to us and the power to even bind and lose with supernatural authority would be given to us to bring the will of God here, on earth as it is in heaven.

Authority over the kingdom of darkness and the responsibility to execute the power of the cross has been given to God's people. This is our inheritance, which comes out of our divine identity as God's sons and daughters. This identity revelation, when understood in its fullness, has a way of revolutionizing our entire life. God's ways will become a part of us and we will live through the lens of sonship, not through the lens of performance, pressure or fear. The gates of hell cannot prevail against a church that truly knows who they are and has decided to operate in the fullness of God's provision.

Personal Application

So what is your name? What is the identity that God has placed upon you? For *every* believer, the foundation of our identity security rests as sons and daughters of our Heavenly Father who loves us and created us to be His beautiful workmanship. Along with that sonship comes a *corporate* mission of bringing the full gospel in powerful manifestations that are *individually* unique and significant. I am first and foremost a *son*, and my identity, beliefs and personality must come forth through that revelation. If not, I will be compelled and driven by the enemy to find security and identity through survival methods driven by fear and insecurity.

A deep root lies beneath the surface in people who struggle with fear and experience a lack of love in their life; *they do not know who they really are.* Because of that, fear has an open door to invade the insecure walls of their identity. The Bible shows us that our identity is found in being God's child. We are *first* His sons and daughters.

Our primary identities are not athletes, presidents, parents, preachers, or elders. Those are simply roles, responsibilities and callings. But if we are not careful, we will place our identity on those titles, while forgetting who we really are. In addition, when those responsibilities or roles become threatened, removed or altered, our lives can become a shattered mess. Stability comes when we understand who we are and walk firmly in it.

If you are at a place where fear seems to continually find cracks to move in, I exhort you to seek your Heavenly Father and ask Him to reveal His love for you and your identity in Him so you can have greater security in your walk. Ask Him to help you develop a strong foundation of security that cannot be shaken by storms or threats.

A Father's Approval

While Jesus was being baptized in water, we hear God the Father splitting the skies with His voice. As He speaks, you hear the Almighty Father echoing and gushing over His Son, by saying, "This is my beloved Son, in whom I am well pleased." In the gospels, God the Father speaks audibly only three times in recorded Scripture. Of those three occurrences, two of the times He utters the phrase, "This is my beloved Son, in whom I am well pleased."[1]

Following this baptism in water and confirmation from His Father, Jesus is led into the wilderness to be tempted by satan. This time of fasting and testing would precede the initiation of His public ministry. During each of the three temptations, He is tempted by satan to give into the lust of the flesh, the lust of the eyes and the pride of life. Interestingly, satan initiates each lure of enticement with a statement of doubt regarding Jesus' identity as God's Son. He begins by asking, "*If* you are the *Son* of God . . . "

The three temptations were all based on questioning and doubting who Jesus was. If satan could get Jesus to doubt and become insecure in His identity, then it would allow for the temptation to take root. And if Jesus needed the Father's approval to maintain a secure identity, then so do you and I.

Fake ID's

A solid personal identity founded on God's love and approval of us is a powerful lock to keep the enemy's lies and weapons at bay. For a number of years, I served as a staff pastor over a worship and music ministry in a fairly large church. One of the things I emphasized to the choir, musicians, and technical people was the solid foundation of having a sure identity through Christ as God's sons and daughters.

This was especially applicable in worship ministry. If you are serving in the music ministry with an identity of a soloist rather than a son or daughter of God, you open yourself up for jealousy, fear, competition, political games, gossip, and rejection. Being a son of God is based on God's approval and His assignments. Having an identity as a soloist allows you to be threatened by anyone else who can sing better than you. What ends up happening is political strategies and divisive games enter as people strive to keep "their position."

Jesus' identity was Messiah, Son of the Living God. You could not move Him from that and He left us an example to follow in His steps. As His people, it is eternally imperative to walk the journey of finding who God made us to be. If the devil tempted Jesus in His identity, than he will certainly use every weapon in his arsenal to question it in your life. You will be subject to other people's expectations and desires, and you will be tempted to develop a fake ID—a mask of identity that covers the real you.

As you walk the process of becoming free from fear, God will begin to open up the eyes of your heart so that you can see who He has called you to be from the foundations of the earth. You are His son. You are His daughter. Seek to be firm in that, because your Daddy has abundant plans of richness for His children.

In addition to that identity, God has unique callings and responsibilities that He will place upon your life. If you are bound up by fear, those callings have the potential to become diluted and dormant. True power in this world will come through the manifestation of the sons of God who stand firm in their identity and spiritual inheritance. If God be for us, who can be against us!

The journey of finding out who God made you to *be* many times begins by removing what you are *not*. This not only takes place by developing a strong spirit, but also in renewing your soul.

---

[1] The three references for God the Father speaking in the gospels are Matthew 3:17, Matthew 17:5 and John 12:28

Chapter 14

Soul Work:
Renewing of the Mind

. . . be transformed by the renewing of your mind . . .
Romans 12:2

When we take spiritual authority over fear and begin to remove its power from our lives, we then have a regular responsibility to continually renew our minds with the power of God's Word and His way of thinking. The mind, as a part of our soul, needs to be renewed and aligned with what God's Word says about us. Spiritual deliverance and freedom not only have a "spirit-man" renewal component, they also have a soul-renewal process as well that is essential.

The word *soul* in the New Testament is the Greek word *psychē*, and speaks mostly of our psychology, way of thinking, identity and memory. Most of what the Bible describes as the soul has to do with our thinking. The mind must be renewed and subjected to what God says about us.

Yet for many, renewing the mind has been very challenging because the spiritual torment they experienced on a spirit level was unrelenting in causing distress within them. A spirit of fear had trained them to submit to fear's thoughts and impulses, thus keeping them from their full spiritual authority. Once deliverance takes place, the back seat driver that seemed to nag and torture is out of the picture and renewing of the mind is not only more possible, but necessary.

The exciting possibility is that at this stage, a true spirit-soul-body makeover is in process. Soul renewal kicks sanctification into higher gears because it involves renewing poor thought patterns, changing personality traits that were developed by fear and cultivating new habits of thinking, believing, and behaving.

This is crucial to understand: even though the spirit is removed from tormenting you, there is still heavy mind programming that needs to be changed and renewed. This is certainly a process, but one that if given time, will help you to turn the corner on fear, phobias, panic, anxiety, stress and worry and walk into greater wholeness.

The Apostle John understood the power of a renewed soul and its effects on human health and prosperous living:

Beloved, I pray that you may prosper in all things and be in health, just as
your soul prospers.
3 John 1:2 (NKJV)

As we learn to develop a soul/mind that has learned to think according to God's ways, we will find a path leading us to prosperity in all things and a life filled with health and restoration. As your soul goes, so does the rest of you.

How Does Renewing the Mind Take Place?

The Apostle Paul gives us a wonderful revelation of what needs to take place in the mind of the believer.[1] This is where the rubber meets the road in order for victory over fear to become a regular way of life.

(For the weapons of our warfare are not carnal, but mighty through God to
the pulling down of strong holds;) Casting down imaginations, and every
high thing that exalteth itself against the knowledge of God, and bringing
into captivity every thought to the obedience of Christ.
2 Corinthians 10:4-5

Through the unction of the Holy Spirit, Paul was able to impart to the church an understanding of where our battle is and how to overcome. In Ephesians we also see an unveiling truth, showing us that we do not wrestle against any humans, but against spiritual architects and rulers who desire to wage war against us from an unseen realm[2]. Paul points out in 2 Corinthians 10:4-5 that the ongoing wrestling which takes place in our mind is spiritual, but he also points out the soul/mind components that are involved in the battle as well. He also emphasizes that our big God has given us the equipping necessary to actually pull down strongholds that the enemy attempts to set up in our lives.

Now, what are strongholds? Strongholds are arenas of thought and reasoning that have been set up within us by the enemy to establish sin and us bound from moving forward in a certain area. It seems from the context of Scripture here that Paul is speaking of spiritual beings that seek to perpetuate the kingdom of satan and sin in the lives of humanity through *a process of thought*. High things speak of wicked beings who seek to exalt themselves above God and bring about imaginations (reasonings and thoughts) of wickedness.

Once the thought is received, the enemy has a greater ability to manifest itself in this world through the person who allowed it. As we discussed earlier, thought comes from the enemy on a spiritual level, but it further becomes a way of programmed thinking in the soul, once a person comes into consistent conformity. The more this happens over time, the more a stronghold becomes solidified.

So how do we fight against these thoughts in the realm of our mind? We discussed earlier the power of taking authority over fear *spiritually* through repentance, authority and deliverance. We now arrive at the day to day discipline of soul work, which the Scriptures certainly do not skip over but give us plenty to arm ourselves with.

Renewed Transformation

The job of mind renewal is the responsibility of every believer, and I have found it to be an area of dynamic breakthrough in my life. Once a spirit of fear is being defeated, it is now also time to renew those places that were once tormented by fear with God's love, truth and power. For example, a person who struggles with the fear of tomorrow needs to be renewed with a revelation that God *holds* tomorrow. As this is renewed in the mind, it makes room for a lifestyle without worry. This allows a capacity within a person to think about how much God will take care of them rather than worrying that tomorrow will be a tragedy. It is the power of divine renewal.

The person who has struggled with anxiety needs to daily renew his mind that God the Father has his back and will continue to work on his behalf as he rests in His love. Those who have social anxieties need to replace those recordings and memories with thoughts and experiences that reveal God's love, care and protection through all their social interactions. Those who fight with phobias must allow themselves to renew those phobic thought patterns with a revelation that God has not given them a spirit of fear. He will not leave you hanging and will carry you through with His love and grace. Truly the revelation of God's Word must now be *experienced*, so that personal life transformation can take effect.

Take <u>Every</u> Thought Captive

Taking every thought captive has been something that many have heard, but have found difficult to practice and maintain. Over time, many lose heart and do not maintain this vital spiritual practice. It is one that cannot be ignored or bypassed. Mind renewal is essential for every believer who seeks to walk in God's ways, because walking in His ways requires Kingdom *thinking*. In renewing the mind and maintaining a renewed mind, taking every thought captive is the key. And when the Word says take *every* thought captive, He means *every* thought!

This means that even when you receive a thought from the Lord, you have been given permission to take it captive and hold it to the lens of God's Word and His ways. God's voice will not violate His Word. He may violate your faulty understanding of His Word, but that is a whole other subject in itself. God is not insecure and will not become offended if you take His thoughts captive. The thoughts of God are filled with so much love and power that as we grow in Him, we won't be able to miss Him when He speaks anyway! In fact, as you walk out of fear, you will learn to become more accustomed to hearing and knowing the voice of the Holy Spirit.

Many believers get lost in this whole concept, because they believe every thought that comes at them like a wave *must* be from God. Yet the Scriptures teach us that satan comes as an angel of light and would love to bring about torment through agreement with ungodly thoughts or words of divination.

Many times impressions will come that seem to line up with God's Word, but are filled with condemnation, lies, fear and other spirits of deception. These deviant thoughts are filled with murky waters and can lead us to walking in error. This is where many cults and perverted sects can begin to form. If this is the case, there may be an antichrist spirit seeking to bring defilement with beliefs and statements that do not line up with God's Word or His view of you as His child.

Satan knows God's words very well and can even use the Scripture against you, using accusation, guilt, shame and condemnation. He can take something from the Word and twist it in a way to make you feel afraid and tormented. That is why it is crucial that we become more than familiar with what God says about us through His Word.

Seeing these attacks and perversions should not scare us from desiring to hear from God. He longs to speak to His children and reveal Himself in these days. Our word of caution simply needs to be that of arming ourselves against the polluted waters of deception that seek to prevent us from receiving a pure witness from the Holy Spirit or guidance from His voice. Do not flee from hearing the voice of God as you seek to remove fear. In fact, the more you become free, the more diligent you should be to seek the promptings and leadings of God. He speaks through a myriad of ways and we ought to be open receptors of those signals.

On a personal note, when I began to get free from fear, I found that I had a much more open hard drive to receive the voice of the Lord and hear His direction, yet I had to make an intentional decision to allow Him to talk where fear had spoken for so many years. In your deliverance, do not walk away from listening to possible promptings from God. Remember that satan can only pervert or distort. He cannot create, so he uses fear to keep us confused and locked out of being able to hear God's direction. Fear wants to keep you from dreaming and it wants to hold you back from receiving visions and dreams of greatness. It is time that we take back that ground for what God really meant for us!

Listening to the Right Thoughts

Our sense of hearing needs to be tuned to a much greater degree, mainly because so many have become accustomed to listening to fear, living it and justifying its work in their life. Sometimes people can even take their actions and give credit to God when in fact they were driven by a spirit of fear. I have heard more times than I can remember people throwing around the phrase "God told me to . . . " like it is a statement we can just flip around without care or thought.

Sadly enough, many of these actions were credited to God, but were actually driven by fear. I have even witnessed people saying that God told them to be afraid or that He used fear as a tool to teach them. I even remember times when I did this myself. Others like me in the past have made decisions based on an anxious gut, thinking that God must be behind it since the impressions were so intense. What we end up with instead of greater glory is increased torment and insanity.

Personal Honesty

Again, I have to emphasize, I do not want you to go into fear about hearing God's voice and worrying that you will be deceived by a spirit of error. My utmost desire is for you to become free from fear, anxiety and stress in *all* areas of your life. In fact I am finding that the more I get free from fear and seek to tune in to God; I am coming to a place of paradox that does not seem to bother me as much anymore. Let me explain.

I have to be very honest. Many times I do not *really* know if it is God speaking to me or not. I am learning to get better tuned and to get my frequency range tweaked every day. My goal is to be able to live in constant communion with His presence and His voice. I am growing in it. The only difference is, I am not as afraid to fail, so I step out in faith to stir up gifts and to trust what I sense He is saying. But I refuse to fall into guilt, fear, regret or double mindedness over it. As I grow, I begin to develop a discerning of spirits, to see what is really behind the thoughts and motivations of my life. That is why getting the Word of God in us is so important.

If fear is operating, then I will live in panic of missing what God says, misinterpreting what I think He is saying, and will live a confusing double-minded life. Yet on the contrary, I can choose to take what I am hearing, line it up with the word of God and see how it filters through God's heavenly lens. On that basis, I need to make my decisions. And above all this, I must remember and ponder this thought: God's got my back. He'll take care of me. I do not have to live in fear that I will not make the right decision or I'll miss what He is saying. I don't have to cower in the corner when intimidation comes against me. I know I have a Father in heaven who has got me covered. If I make a wrong decision, He will show me and lead me in paths of righteousness. That is true freedom, and it feels so great!

Wake Up and Take Charge

I am going to get very practical with you in these pages, so tune in carefully. As you approach freedom from fear, you cannot take a backseat approach, as this is not simply a defensive work. As a believer, you have a divine duty to daily initiate an offensive attack by taking charge of what happens in your mind. *In other words, you need to make a consistent determination of what you are going to think about.* Thousands of believers need to end the habit of waking up each morning in passivity, waiting for what that day presents as a foundation for establishing their atmosphere of thinking. That is a defeated mentality which is a sure setup for failure. Instead, choose to face every day with a resolve to establish your thought life. This is not something that you can depend on someone else to do, but it must be personally developed.

Begin your morning in the Bible or with music playing that edifies your spirit (In fact, seek to close your day the same way). Take time to start immediately speaking to yourself. Turn some worship music on. Begin to take initiative by thinking about those things which are honoring to God and meditate on thoughts that work against the tactics of fear. Think and speak those things that God has promised to do in your life in anticipation for them to happen. You once thought down the lines of fear's thinking. Now it is time to think about matters of faith and let God show you the great things He has in store for you. Start off the day purposefully by thinking, "Today is a new day. I am going to face it with God and I am going to overcome. Great things are in store." Develop a practice of thinking that allows you to dream big for what God can do in your life and will usher in God's peace to flow over your mind.

As I have been writing this book, God has helped to put this into regular practice. I have been waking up with a different perspective for a while now, speaking these anticipatory words, saying, "What are you going to do today Lord?!" I have been deeply convicted by God that if I am going to be a continual overcomer, it will be predicated on being filled with the anticipation of God working miracles, healings, signs and wonders in my life. That godly expectation is a breeding ground for God to work above and beyond our wildest dreams. It gives Him the soil of faith to bring an abundant harvest into our lives. I am learning to kick off each day with this kind of faith-building eagerness that invites the presence and power of God to perform great feats in my life.

I encourage you to find a way to do this yourself. You can start off today. Even if you do not see drastic results right away, spiritual momentum will eventually kick in and send you soaring. I am a living testimony of this. Start off your day commanding your body, soul and spirit to come in line with the Word of God and the anointing of the Holy Spirit. You may start some days off without believing it or feeling it, but those words will still have an effect, I promise. Seek to open up your heart to the good things of God, rather than letting the enemy and your flesh steer you into negative focus and heaviness. Have expectancy for your Daddy to do great things in your life. I have witnessed this time and again. I know if He will do it for me, He will certainly do it for you too.

Test the Spirits

The Bible tells us in 1 John 4 to test the spirits to see if they are from God. This is not something to be afraid of, causing us to run and hide from everything. Nor is it meant for us to be clouded with religiousness, leading us to be critical of everything we see. This is a part of your spiritual arsenal towards possessing and maintaining victory. This is a tool of being sober and alert to what is *not* of God that is trying to influence your way of thinking and living.

Your enemy has deceitful methods, and it is critical that we are not ignorant of satan's devices. With that in mind, there are thoughts that can sneak in from a spirit realm that are not of God, and I feel it is important to share a few of them with you here. These all love to partner with fear and keep you from a renewed mind that is free.

The Instability of Double-Mindedness

Double-mindedness is a colleague of fear, because it supports the paranoia that enters when we are not confident in our decision making. The Scriptures teach us that severe instability will surely follow the person who is not firmly single minded in his decisions.[3] This confusion and double-mindedness sneaks in very easily if a believer is not sure of who they are in Christ as a child of God. Double-mindedness must be attacked through confidence in your identity. In addition, defeating this comes when you make an allowance for yourself to make mistakes. It is an unrealistic pressure to expect yourself to make perfect and absolutely precise decisions *every* single time. It only adds to fear's pressures anyway. You must give room for yourself to know that your Daddy loves you and will help you in your journey as you submit to Him.

Jesus pointed out the severity of double-mindedness when he said in Luke 9:62, "No man, having put his hand to the plough, and looking back, is fit for the kingdom of God." Part of your spiritual fitness is being strong in spirit, knowing that God has placed His trust in you to serve Him and make right decisions. For many of you, He trusts you more than you even trust yourself.

Paul admonished the body of Christ when he gave this life changing revelation to the Philippians by saying, "forgetting those things which are behind and reaching forward to those things which are ahead."[4] Staying locked in your past decisions for the most part only brings torment, usually insane torment, because you were never meant to make a choice and then spend your days rehashing that moment. As a believer, make it your aim to please the Father in everything that you do. In the meantime, allow yourself to be wide open for God to bring conviction in your life.

Guilt and Condemnation

Guilt and condemnation are not from God and they do not originate from His Kingdom. Yet many times they disguise themselves to resemble godly correction and chastisement; which can add a higher state of torment to the person who is bound with this. The desire of guilt and condemnation is to get you to live with an extreme sense of shame and regret, so that you cannot experience God's love and forgiveness.

Guilt causes an emotional and mental spiral as you end up focusing on how "guilty" you are, as if standing before a legalistic judge. Most of the time guilt will point to an issue that should not even be brought to the surface; often areas that we have released to God's forgiveness. Guilt will lead people to believe that they are not forgiven and will accuse a person into feelings of unworthiness and unlovingness.

Many religions and denominations use guilt as a way of motivating people to conform to their sacred patterns or to contribute to their cause. Unfortunately, it can be very successful because guilt can certainly motivate a crowd. Yet there is no freedom, love or patience in that way of living. Guilt is dangerous to use in the church and it is deadly to apply in relationships anywhere. It will create interactions where people will constantly keep score instead of giving and receiving love and forgiveness in freedom. In the age of grace that we live in, we must allow God's love to dominate and make room for our spiritual discernment to remove guilt as a tool in our circles.

Condemnation is a counterfeit that communicates disapproval from God or from a spiritual authority that has a great deal of influence in a person's life. Unless dealt with, condemnation will cause any person to live as though they cannot access God's presence or love throughout their life. Condemnation will work to keep you from being rooted in the the radical love of God.

I find that many people who fall into an action of sin also end up falling into guilt and condemnation, where true freedom is not found. When these counterfeits are present, repentance is not good enough—one must go through penance to come back to wholeness. This can last hours, days or even a lifetime. Interestingly, this happens many times with people who have sensitive hearts and have an intense desire to please God. The enemy has taken this precious heart and has sought to destroy this child of God with an accusing spirit of guilt and condemnation.

The solution for this bondage is to develop a greater sense of discernment and allow for God's love to flood in. We must walk in a revelation that God is *for* us and He does not walk around in constant anger against His children. He loves us. He is so willing to speak to us and direct us. And He will do it with extravagant love. Remember, God loves all those that He corrects. When He brings correction to His child, it is always done through His identity of love and through the finished work of Christ.

To the believer, when you feel God's correction, you should also feel His love at the same time. If thoughts and impressions come bringing a great deal of replay into the past with feelings of shame, then I will guarantee that something in the transmission is not from God. Here are some verses to reinforce your battle against guilt and condemnation.

He has not dealt with us according to our sins, nor punished us according to our iniquities. For as the heavens are high above the earth, So great is His mercy toward those who fear Him; As far as the east is from the west, So far has He removed our transgressions from us.
Psalms 103:10-12 (NKJV)

There is therefore now no condemnation to them which are in Christ Jesus, who walk not after the flesh, but after the Spirit.
Romans 8:1

For God sent not his Son into the world to condemn the world; but that the world through him might be saved.
John 3:17

When Jesus had raised Himself up and saw no one but the woman, He said to her, "Woman, where are those accusers of yours? Has no one condemned you?" She said, "No one, Lord." And Jesus said to her, "Neither do I condemn you; go and sin no more."
John 8:10-11 (NKJV)

For if ye turn again unto the LORD, your brethren and your children shall find compassion before them that lead them captive, so that they shall come again into this land: for the LORD your God is gracious and merciful, and will not turn away his face from you, if ye return unto him.
2 Chronicles 30:9

The Quicksand of Self-Pity

If guilt and condemnation major in focusing on your rear view mirror, then self-pity has the doctoral degree on your negative past. Self pity will not allow you to move forward because it acts as a quicksand; locking you into your past and creating an inability for you to gain freedom and deliverance. It causes you to believe that you are hopeless and will never be able to move out of your dysfunctions and bondages. Self-pity will link arms with fear, rejection, condemnation and depression to propel you into a place of long-term defeat.

In ministering to people, I have found it difficult seeing men and women healed and delivered when a strong spirit of self-pity is present. This spirit will bind the person to the past, causing them to feel that they will never move forward. Tapes of past wounds and hardships replay in endless cycles. No manner of arguing or coercing helps until the individual personally comes to grips *with* and repents *for* coming into agreeing with that self-pity.

You can discern that the quicksand of self-pity is present in your life when you display a consistent habit of not heeding the words of encouragement from others who seek to minister to you and add hope to your walk. This is when you have to ask yourself, "Do I really *want* to be healed and delivered, or do I actually *like* the despair I am in and prefer to remain in this 'stuff'?"

A good example of self-pity is well illustrated in John chapter 5 when Jesus came to the pool of Bethesda and asked a man with an infirmity for 38 years, "Do you *want* to be made well?" The sick man's answer is astounding, because He doesn't reply to the question, but instead, focuses on his problematic history. In verse 7 this man's response is narrowly fixed on the reasons *why* he thinks healing has not occurred, even though his Solution is standing right in front of him.

The sick man answered Him, "Sir, I have no man to put me into the pool when the water is stirred up; but while I am coming, another steps down before me."
John 5:7 (NKJV)

Fortunately for this man, Jesus ignored the self-pity and healed him in His compassion, grace and mercy for the man. Yet the lessons in this passage ought to be sobering for us today. In our current culture, the trap of self-pity is easily camouflaged and must be recognized, or else a spiritual spiral can induce a person into a despair that will not allow love or care to penetrate. Major breakthrough will arrive to the one who will not let the enemy deceive them into feeling sorry for them self, for that only leads to greater depression and hopelessness. Victory is around the corner for the one who *repents* of that pity and stands strong in spirit to pursue wholeness. I cannot break this for you. It must be broken by a heart-felt decision to stand up and receive the delivering power and love from God the Father and others around you.

In my research regarding real life quicksand, I have noticed that the only true way to get out of it is to calmly shed excess weight, start looking and leaning forward, slowly pull yourself to solid ground and inch your way out. It can be done.

Live By What You Know – Not Just How You Feel

As you take a journey away from fear and move towards faith and the love of God, renewing the mind involves making a firm decision to continually live by what you know in Christ, not by how you feel—no matter how bad things may seem at times. During your path to victory, fear will come by and see what is happening in your life—to check if you are vulnerable to its tactics. As you approach certain experiences, sometimes fear will project the anxiety you had the last time you approached this same moment in the past. Fear, anxiety, hot flashes, panic and worry will all try to kick up and tell you that you never got free and are in complete bondage again. It is critical that during this time you practice what I call a "renewed experience" with that old occurrence that used to invoke fear. It is during this time that pushing through this situation by what you know in your heart through God's Word is critical. It is through practicing God's power in circumstances like this, combined with the knowledge of His love, which will bring you to a new place of triumph over fear.

When dealing with fear, *do not debate with it*. You do not need to. If you try to rationally fight it, it will find another crack to instigate. Do not engage in arguments with the enemy, but develop renewed patterns of thinking to replace those old recordings of fear that are attempting to creep up. This is spiritual training that takes time, but will build a new you that puts away the old man who was bound with fear.

Choosing *not* to engage with the voice of fear does not mean living in denial either. Those who live in constant denial never truly deal with their problems and dysfunctions. What I am saying is that we need to face our fears and walk through them, without looking back and without debating with fear about the future. For some, walking away from fear may seem like living in denial, *because fear was their reality*. Many have been bound so deeply by fear that it became a rooted part of their life that effected their speech and actions. Beating fear involves no longer engaging with the nonsense that it has been spewing out.

It is time for us to make some drastic changes and for a spiritual paradigm shift to come into our relationships, workplaces, homes and churches. When we stop listening to everything fear says, you will see people with more power and boldness rising up to take some awesome risks for God. The tables will be turned on what fear was trying to do all along.

The "Gut" Voice

In making decisions, too many, including Christians, get driven by their "gut" or their instincts. This practice involves making decision after decision based on that abstract arena of feeling, hoping that it will prove itself faithful in the end. All it takes is for that "gut" to prove itself correct once, and people will lay down their lives in obedience to that voice. For Christians, we may attribute our "gut" to God's voice, which is not always the case, and it is can be a very dangerous value system for making decisions.

The Bible says there are many voices, and none without significance.[5] Developing a discernment to know when the voice of fear is speaking can be extremely helpful in developing strength and maturity. In doing so, please understand this reality: *fear has a very loud voice!* It speaks loudly and communicates a sense of panic and urgency that must be focused on immediately. This is not to be confused with the fight or flight that comes over your body when you see a car coming at you in the street. This is addressing the voice that comes with a spirit of fear. With obedience to this voice comes drivenness, striving, instability and uneasiness because fear has nothing to offer but torment.

The voice of God is not just a loud voice. Many believers interpret the loudest voice they hear to be the voice of God when many times it is not the case. The Bible speaks about the voice of God being a still small voice. His voice can thunder. It can shake the mountains and move the earth. But He speaks to His beloved in a voice that is loving, guiding, and in line with His Word. Whenever God spoke in the Scriptures, there was no question that He spoke. The only time that there was doubt is when it came from people who just wanted to criticize and had no desire to see the face of God. (That is a whole other topic indeed.)

God's voice brings with it authority, clarity and presence, but there is a stillness to it like none other. This cannot be described in human words, but if you have experienced it, you know what I am talking about. His voice adds to our faith and brings us comfort. His words bring a true godly peace that leads us on a journey into righteousness. Even when He is correcting us, there is still something very loving and special about that voice.

God's voice is still and loving, but I have learned that *He will not compete with the other voices that clamor for your attention.* He will have no other gods before him, and if fear is your god, it will be the voice that you receive when the rubber meets the road.

Make God's Thinking – Your Thinking

For many of you reading this book, fear has been talking to you since you were an infant. For many it has been inherited through your generations. Your father was fearful. Your mother was a worrier. In addition, *their* parents struggled with fear. Now it has gained momentum in your life as you came into agreement with its thought processes. It may only be in a few areas of your life or possibly thousands. Regardless, you know fear has been driving you like wildfire. I am realizing more and more that so many of my thoughts and actions of the past were motivated by fear, even though I defended myself by saying I was being wise or careful. In actuality, I was listening to fear and became vulnerable because I did not realize in my heart that God loved me and had my back. This has been a process of daily renewal, but it has been one that has grown significantly for me.

Taking every thought captive may seem like a lot of work, but it becomes more second nature as you conform yourself to the image of Christ. This is where continual discipleship is necessary. The problem is that we have had so many areas of fear programming, that we have to begin to address them, many times *one by one*. It may seem overwhelming, but there comes a wave of deliverance momentum that will crash over the schemes of the enemy as you seek to renew your mind according to God's Word. **Do not be discouraged by process.** It is one of God's ways of teaching us to be hard wired in His way of thinking.

Have you ever watched a suspenseful adventure movie a second or third time and noticed that you still feel a little anxious and nervous for the hero in the story, even though you already know the ending? It is the same way with our spiritual walk. We can know the ending, and the ending is good! Yet because of the nature of fear's tactics, we have to be renewed in God's ways of thinking every day. We have to constantly keep our good future and victorious end at the forefront of our attention.

That is why making a commitment to stand on God's Word is so essential. The Word of God needs to become a part of us, so that its power can be activated in our lives. Your values, identity, thoughts, speech and actions need to come out of the Word as it dwells richly in you.

Our thinking can be like that of tuning a piano. When you tune piano strings, the inclination is for those strings over time is to loosen or tighten back to the position they were in before being adjusted. That is why consistent re-tuning is necessary, and this applies directly to your spiritual life as well. You need constant spiritual tuning, which involves tuning your mind to think about faith, hope and love, not fear. This keeps the strings of your mind moving towards an ever increasing spiritual capacity.

It is time to dwell and meditate on all the great plans that God has for you; plans to prosper you, not harm you; plans to give you a good future and a hope.[6] It is from the Scriptures that we can receive this truth and live a renewed experience. This is where we will go in the next chapter.

---

[1] In this writing, there may be those who have not yet received a relationship with God through Jesus Christ. I want to emphasize that a personal relationship with God is necessary for these teachings to really take effect.

[2] Ephesians 6:12

[3] James 1:8

[4] Philippians 3:13 (NKJV)

[5] 1 Corinthians 14:10

[6] Jeremiah 29:11-12

Chapter 15

Untapped Potential: Practicing Godly Meditation

For as he hath thought in his soul, so is he . . .
Proverbs 23:7a (YLT)

Biblical meditation can set us up for God to speak and move supernaturally, because of the spiritual atmosphere that becomes cultivated within our inner man to receive the Word of God and a move of His Holy Spirit.

True godly meditation is at the heart of a victorious Christian walk, and it is a key to setting up an atmosphere for God to speak and move in our life. Meditation works to mold and shape who we are, by laying blocks of what to believe, how to think and how to live. In addition, those things which we chose to focus and dwell on will take form in our lives over time. The Bible teaches that *as you think, so shall you be.*[1]

Godly Meditation vs. New Age Meditation

Unfortunately in this day and age, the word *meditation* has often been stolen by the enemy, who has flooded our society with new age practices of the occult. Those who dabble in these areas are taught to exercise techniques that open them up to channeling evil spirits. These pathways can be dangerous because people end up opening their minds to whatever wants to come in, making room for possible divination and other kinds of evil spirits to enter. Ironically, these methods bring more long term torment than inner peace.

Yet we should never let the counterfeits that exist push us away from true genuine meditation. Meditation was God's design, so that we could contemplate on His Word and open our spirit to connect with Him, who is spirit. Meditation was His idea and we must learn the true power of Christian meditation.

Satan never creates anything. He does not have that power. He can only make polluted counterfeits. We must discern his tactics, but at the same time be confident that God wants to connect with us through our times of meditating on Him.

God never teaches us to carelessly clear our minds and open it up to whatever wants to come in. In fact, we have been given the responsibility to *fill* our minds with His peace and His thoughts. When we meditate on God's Word and His ways, we build an ability within us to ward off attacks of the enemy. In addition, we set ourselves up to receive deeper revelations of God's nature.

The word *revelation* in the Scriptures is a New Testament word meaning to "unveil, disclose, reveal, appear, manifest." The Word of God has the power to manifest and reveal truth to the one who diligently seeks God with all their heart. It is imperative to understand that there is a difference between perusing the Scriptures and receiving the Word in *revelation*. That is why you can read the same Scripture passage ninety-nine times and experience an explosion in your spirit on the hundredth reading. This is what occurs when the Holy Spirit meets a ready heart that desires to receive life-changing truth. When that reality enters in, it has an explosive power that develops into a filter by which we view life. It becomes the catalyst for supernatural power to manifest in our world.

The Living Word of God

What is the Word of God? Many believers forget or do not understand that *Jesus is the Living Word*, which shows us that the Word of God is not just a book, but a living person. The written Scriptures (the Bible) not only contain the Word of God, but they also come from a *source* that originated that Word. Jesus is the eternal Word of God.

To make this clearer, we have to understand the Godhead as communicated throughout the Scriptures; God the Father, God the Son (The Word), and God the Holy Spirit. The Godhead is one, yet three persons as well. This seems like a mystery, yet it is also amazingly simple. As you discover the revelation of the Godhead, you will find an amazing plural unity of God presented throughout the Scriptures.

The Holy Spirit of God seeks to work in the hearts of mankind to lead them to Jesus Christ, who Himself said He came to lead us to the Father. The Holy Spirit has a multifaceted work which includes comfort, guidance, baptism, power, anointing, conviction and many other activities that we could expound upon. The Spirit of God also has a strong work of confirming the work of the Word of God within us as we come to a greater sense of revelation of what God is saying to us and about us.

Jesus is God the Word who came in the flesh as Jesus Christ. He was in existence from the beginning and was present when all things were created. In fact, it was His voice that brought creation into existence. The Holy Spirit hovered over creation, waiting to execute the spoken Word of God over the universe. It is the heart of Father God that is revealed through Jesus Christ and carried out by the work of the Spirit. God the Father thinks it. God the Word speaks it. God the Holy Spirit executes it.

With this understanding, it makes so many passages come alive in the Scriptures. One of the best examples of this is found in Hebrews 4. Notice the places of emphasis, revealing that the Word of God is not just a book, it is a person—the person of Jesus Christ.

For the _word of God_ is quick, and powerful, and sharper than any two edged sword, piercing even to the dividing asunder of soul and spirit, and of the joints and marrow, and _is a discerner_ of the thoughts and intents of the heart.

Neither is there any creature that is not manifest in _his sight_: but all things are naked and opened unto the eyes of _him_ with whom we have to do.

Seeing then that we have a great _high priest_, that is passed into the heavens, _Jesus the Son of God_, let us hold fast our profession.

For we have not an <u>high priest</u> which cannot be touched with the feeling of our infirmities; but <u>was in all points tempted</u> like as we are, yet without sin.
Let us therefore come boldly unto the throne of grace, that we may obtain mercy, and find grace to help in time of need.
Hebrews 4:12-16

True godly meditation is not simply just thinking about memory verses, it comes through a revelation of Jesus Christ, as shown through the Scriptures. The more you receive the Word, the more you understand who Jesus is and the greater you are touched by the heart of the Father, because knowing Jesus will lead you to the Father. Meditation comes through a journey of building precept upon precept as to who God is and who He has called us to be. It is also a set of building blocks that must stand upon a strong foundation.

Chewing the Word

But his delight is in the law of the Lord, And in His law he meditates day and night.
Psalms 1:2 (NKJV)

The psalmist in this Old Testament passage gives us insight into the heart of a man or woman of God. Their first delight is in God's Word and His ways, which leads them to mediate on that Word day and night. This Word becomes a free flowing river that is pondered continually and contemplated on throughout the lifetime a believer.

Biblical meditation is well illustrated in the way certain animals process their food through what is known as "chewing the cud". Certain ruminant animals, like cattle, have an anatomy and process of digestion that is unique to other living creatures. In the example of cattle, they have one stomach, but four chambers within it. Because of this peculiar digestive system, cattle are able to eat certain foods that would normally be non-digestible by regurgitating food back up from the first section of the multi-chambered stomach to be re-chewed. In this state, the regurgitated food is referred to as "cud". Once the food has been slowly masticated for a time, it is then sent back down to the stomach section for further digestion. This process takes place in graduated and repeated cycles.

For the believer, "chewing the cud" spiritually is a process, which if understood and faithfully applied, will bring you to new heights of growth. Too many today want God to touch them quickly and remove all their problems in a flash. In our fast-paced American environment, we look for God to microwave our fears away and give us a nice drive-through car wash of cleansing. I certainly encourage everyone to seek for those dynamic moments where heaven invades earth and our lives are changed by the touch of God. In the meantime, as we pursue those supernatural encounters, we must not despise the "crock pot process" of growth where God teaches us through times of meditating on God's Word, His character and His ways. This practice builds in us our spiritual DNA as we build the blocks of our identity as sons and daughters of God.

This becomes a greater reality when we allow ourselves to receive the implanted Word with patience. As God reveals His Word to you in a way that becomes personally relevant and life-changing, take the time to chew on it. Don't rush on. His words are so powerful that one could spend a lifetime discovering the ramifications found in any one tiny chunk of living revelation. An entire life long investment could be placed on the multiple facets of revelation that can come through one verse like John 3:16. So when God's Word comes in power to your life, allow yourself to park there until He shows you to move on. He may have something there that needs to take its time to become a greater part of you. It may also be the very thing that will break fear's programming and even become a part of your life message. This is that *rhema* word that gets spoken into your heart with divine power.

I encourage you to study God's Word and continually feed your hunger for it. But when God reveals truth in power to you, park yourself there until God unites that knowledge with divine experience and fruit in your life. Truth found in God's Word must meet experience. We were meant and designed to experience God's truth through application. When that occurs, you receive the explosive power of the Word. In addition, God's design for you as well His purposes and plans for your life can be found in greater clarity.

Spiritual Implants

James teaches us to remove those things that are not of God's kingdom and develop a habit of allowing the Word of God to become a part of our entire being.

Therefore lay aside all filthiness and overflow of wickedness, and receive with meekness the implanted word, which is able to save your souls.
James 1:21 (NKJV)

As we remove what is in us that is not of God, those pathways of thinking certainly need to be replaced with truth, which comes from the Word of God. That Word needs to be more than a daily devotional — it must become a part of us. James says we need to receive the *implanted* Word, which is also translated in the King James as "engrafted." Both words help to convey the meaning, which show us that the Word must become rooted within us to such an extent that it becomes a part of our existence. It must be a part of our thinking, right down to our brain neuropathways and synapses.

James tells us that the Word will *save your soul*. That word "save" is the Greek word *sozo*, which has a deep and multifaceted definition. It does not just mean "saved," as in "saved and going to heaven." It speaks of being "saved, delivered, healed, protected" and much more, which conveys the freeing power of Jesus Christ — whose words must dwell in us richly.

As a part of overcoming fear, we are on a journey of developing a life-long habit of getting to know Jesus, the Savior, Lord and Living Word, because we have been called to be conformed into His image. In doing so, we need to let biblical meditation on the Word of God become something that we focus on daily throughout our lives.

It is through faithful godly meditation that previous thoughts focused on fear can be replaced with new thoughts that magnify the good things that God has in store for those who love Him and walk with Him. It can also open up the portals of heaven to pour out supernatural blessings and power into our life. May His Word burn richly in our hearts!

Focusing on a Good Report

When I was young, I remember my parents asking me how my time at school was going. In addition, they would regularly inquire about my studies to ensure I was staying on track with my grades. Many times I would give them the typical answer of "everything's fine" or "my studies are going well". Yet the reality of my progress in school would be clearly revealed by the unquestionable truth given by my report card. This progress report never played any games, and despite my attempts to plead otherwise, the grade markings were not a result of computer error. This report spoke the facts as to my academic activity and gave me the standard by which I was to go by in future semesters.

In our spiritual life, things are a little different, yet there is a similar principle in the illustration: *the report always has an effect on those who receive the news.* Any report, whether good or bad will have a dramatic effect on those who receive it and meditate on it. The report we dwell on can completely change our state of mind, the condition of our spirit and our reactions. It can move our hearts to action or it can bring great devastation and heartache.

With that said, *you must make a decision on whose report you are going to believe.* As you meditate on God's Word, His thoughts will become the report card by which you evaluate yourself and everything around you. My question to you is the same that was asked to Isaiah, *will you believe the report of the Lord?* For if you choose to believe the report of the enemy over your life, you will think and respond accordingly. Yet if you choose to receive God's report about how much He loves you and has great plans for you, you will learn to meditate and act in the ways of faith, hope and love.

Paul gave us the framework in Philippians by which we should evaluate every single thought that we meditate on.

Finally, brethren, whatsoever things are true, whatsoever things are honest, whatsoever things are just, whatsoever things are pure, whatsoever

things are lovely, whatsoever things are of good report; if there be any
virtue, and if there be any praise, think on these things.
Philippians 4:8

Do you see the parameters? Do you notice that most of what he lists here is not what many people spend their time meditating on? For numerous folks, the majority of the day is spent uncovering any possibility of doom, failure, or evil that surrounds them or could surround them. Yet Paul says, we should only meditate and act on thoughts that fit under this filter:

1. **True:** Not concealing or washing over things. That includes removing yourself from gossip that is sent your way or any kind of forecasted statement of potential lies. Rely on the Holy Spirit to lead you into *all* truth.

2. **Honest:** Meditations that develop character and uprightness, where you foster actions and relationships surrounded by honesty, integrity and love.

3. **Just:** This speaks of thoughts that lead you towards holiness and righteousness in your character and identity. This is a practice of developing greater light in your meditations that drive darkness away.

4. **Pure:** Developing meditation and thought patterns that focus on pure thoughts that promote modesty and spiritual cleanliness. Not thoughts of lust, bitterness, jealousy, fear, rejection, strife, etc.

5. **Lovely:** A thought pattern that teaches you to look for the best in people around you and to diligently search to find loveliness in every situation that you are in. Putting on this cloak of Phileo love (affectionate love from the heart) creates an atmosphere that extends love towards others and makes them feel accepted.

6. **Good Report:** This speaks of meditating on reputable information that comes from sources that are reliable and well spoken of. Does that mean you ignore bad news that is true? No. What it means is that we are to wait for the reliable truth to arrive, usually from the person closest to the situation or the one that is in the situation. Learn to think about that circumstance the way God would. A practice of seeking a good

report involves staying away from meditating on gossip or slander regarding anyone, including reports brought against you.

7. **Virtue:** This must be added to develop your faith[2]. Virtue is what can be released in moments of ministry[3]. You give out what you have received, and in God's virtue lies dynamic power to minister to people's lives. Virtue speaks of divine goodness and power as well. Meditate and dwell on the great power of God that dwells in you richly.

8. **Praise:** This word speaks of a narration or story that presents God and His greatness. This is where it becomes critical to spend time meditating on the testimony of what God is doing in the land. A heart filled with praise is usually also filled with gratitude, focusing on what God has done and is going to do — not on what we think He has *not* done.

Don't just wait for a bad thought from fear to come your way so that you can fend it off. Develop a spiritual practice and take the constant initiative to fill your mind with meditations and contemplations that line up with the Kingdom of God. With this practice you will build a fortress that cannot be invaded by your enemy. Proverbs 15:30 tells us that a good report makes your bones fat. Strengthen yourself in the Word of God and meditate on it daily, as it brings great stature and posture to your whole being.

I Am Done With Introspection

There are a pocket of people who need to receive this just as I did: *Introspection is going to have to cease in order for us to achieve greater sanity and wholeness.* I have found that introspection also does nothing to aid our development in learning to meditate on the things of God. Within the lines of learning to break fear, introspection is a tool of the enemy because it promotes an incessant habit of inward observation and examination of one's own mental and emotional state, with the intent of trying to figure out issues and fix them. This never produces long term results, nor does it assist in the fight against the workings of fear. In addition, introspection is not a scriptural concept. Its focus is on the past failures, which God never tells us to dwell on.

God brings us through transformation when we come into contact with His truth and love. On the other hand, introspection is constantly turning up every stone and pulling back every issue of the past, trying to find a key into the future, when what is usually found is more accusation, guilt, condemnation, self-pity, regret, and fear. Unfortunately, this has become a habit for many and has turned into a religious routine that has kept people looking in the rear view mirror while sitting in neutral.

With the encouragement that Paul gave to the Philippians, I exhort you to forget *those things which are behind* and reach forward *to those things which are ahead*[4]. We need to let go of that bondage of introspection and release ourselves into a life of freedom, especially in the mind.

Recently, I read where an author addressed his battle with introspection and wrote a prayer letter to let go of that nasty habit. It touched my heart and gave me revelation that took me to another level. As I received the heart behind his letter, I took the prayer and made it my own.[5] Here is my personal version.

Heavenly Father,

I know that I don't do so well when I look inward and try to search under every bush and between every crack for a possible fault in me or in my past. So I am going to stop that because it is causing me to lose my stability in you and it is keeping me from walking in your rest. I make a firm decision to watch over my heart with diligence, so that it is always tender towards You and towards people. I commit myself to staying in your Word continually, knowing that it is a sword, and I open up my life for that sword to cut me deeply. Expose those things that are not pleasing to you and bring revelation where I have been walking in ignorance. In doing so, give me the grace and love that will empower me to forsake sin and walk in truth. I also commit myself to come before You daily and develop a lifestyle that walks with an awareness of Your presence. Your Word and presence is like a fire. Let it have a consuming work in my life to burn those things which are not pleasing to You and to build an undying passion within me for You and Your ways. I want my heart and identity to be more like Jesus. Be merciful to me in those things. I also make a commitment to stay in fellowship with Your people. Iron sharpens iron. I expect you to "anoint the words of a friend" to bring me to my senses when I am resistant towards You. Please use these tools to shape my life until Jesus alone and the Father's presence is seen in me. I believe that You have given me Your Spirit and Your heart. I rely on the guidance and comfort of the Holy Spirit to fill me and lead me into all truth. With that said, I turn from introspection and release my life into a journey of pressing forward in confidence and boldness because I am Your child.

Your Son,

Mark

Choose to Remember

I remember the days of old; I meditate on all thy works; I muse on the work of thy hands.
Psalms 143:5

If you are tempted to meditate on the negative past, there is something that is helpful when recalling past events: *choose only to meditate on the works of God's hands in your life and in the lives of those around you.* Meditating on this builds your faith to know that God can and will do it again. In fact, He will perform it in even greater measure! Remember, fear projects doom and gloom into the future and uses the past many times as a reference. Turn the tables by bringing up the works of God in the past that brought salvation, healing, deliverance and help in times of need. Move forward with faith and boldness, knowing that God will bring you to victory.

The Scriptures tell us that the testimony of Jesus is the spirit of prophecy. In other words, the testimony of what God has done in your life through Jesus Christ ushers in the spirit of prophecy to make way for that kind of supernatural work to take place again, especially in the environments where that testimony is given. That is the God-given power of your testimony! As the Lord brings you to new levels of victory, no matter how small you think it is, use it as a stepping stone of faith to help you climb higher, remind you of God's faithfulness in the past and see the work of God manifest again in your future.

David did this when He approached Goliath. Amongst all the doubt, unbelief and fear that was in the camp of God's people, David stood up and declared his testimony that made way for his next level of victory.

David said moreover, "The LORD that delivered me out of the paw of the lion, and out of the paw of the bear, he will deliver me out of the hand of this Philistine . . ."

1 Samuel 17:37

David chose to remember the past victories which became spiritual launching pads, propelling him into victory against his next giant. This was his pattern of living, even in the most difficult of circumstances. David made a solid determination to meditate on the Lord's ways to change His perspective and cause a greater level of courage and boldness to be unleashed in his life.

. . . David encouraged himself in the LORD his God.

1 Samuel 30:6

What is your past victory? What do you have coming against you? Remember the works of God and the wonders of His hands, for He has not left you stranded, but is there in your time of need. Let it be a part of your continual reflection and meditation.

Muttering Sounds

In Psalm 1, the word *meditate* is applied by the godly man in his continual hunger to ponder on the Word of God. Yet the meaning of this word is so much richer than just pondering or thinking. *Meditate*, as used in the Old Testament, speaks of *a muttering or groaning*. It also means *to moan, growl and utter*, which presents a mental picture of a person pacing back and forth, mumbling precepts from the Word out loud over and over again until it is settled firmly within. Truth takes root when it is personally understood, and it often takes a little mumbling and wrestling to get there. Through "muttering," revelation has an opportunity to take shape in a person's life. In order for that to happen, one must develop a lifestyle of biblical meditation, to the point that the passionate moaning over truth becomes understood within.

As you receive the implanted Word, I encourage you to meditate on those truths and open up your heart to receive life-change from the Living Word Himself. Take back the process of meditation which the devil has stolen from so many, and let the power of God's Word set you up for encounters and experiences with His power, love and grace. Do not see those times of mutterings as tedious; view them as breakthrough opportunities for heaven to bust loose in your life.

In order for meditation to connect itself with your freedom, it will have to link arms with the words that are spoken in your life. This is where your mouth comes into play, which is what we will address in the next chapter.

---

[1] Proverbs 23:7
[2] 2 Peter 1:5
[3] Luke 6:19
[4] Philippians 3:13 (NKJV)
[5] Materials from "The Supernatural Ways of Royalty", by Bill Johnson and Kris Vallotton, copyright 2006 used by permission of Destiny Image Publishers, 167 Walnut Bottom Road, Shippensburg, PA 17257 www.destinyimage.com

Chapter 16

Spiritual Mouthwash: Kingdom Speaking

Death and life are in the power of the tongue: and they that love it shall eat the fruit thereof.
Proverbs 18:21

The devil understands the power of the tongue and uses fear to try and remove your ability to speak with love and boldness.

I believe the time has long come for those of us in the body of Christ to take a deeper responsibility for our words. Too often we have remained passive in silence, waiting for someone else to speak forth words of faith, hope and love to our generation. Yet God has deliberately designed our mouths with incredible authority and potent potential so that the work of His Kingdom can be established here on earth. Our words were meant to accomplish God's eternal purposes, from moving mountains that stand before us, to delivering words of exhortation for those who will listen and receive. Unfortunately too many times that strong verbal potential is left dormant in people's lives, or is used to execute works of darkness.

Those who have battled fear-based issues have quietly cowered back while fear has pushed them against the wall, choking their ability to unleash the power of life that is in their tongue. At times when words are able to come forth, instead of speaking of a confident and hopeful future, their words bring emphasis and validation to the workings of fear, doubt, unbelief, anxiety, stress and worry. For those who have sat in silence, it is time to sound the alarm and rise up against fear through speaking with authority the truth of God's Word with boldness. For others who have been programmed to speak endless words of fear, a much needed change and reversal needs to take effect with their verbal expressions. God's Word needs to be established in our hearts, and we must not hesitate to let it come forth from our mouths in love and boldness.

Far too many have been in the wilderness; talking about the good ol' days, complaining about the daily struggles and verbally validating their fears and worries. This all must end if we are going to attack the kingdom of fear and walk in victory. I am praying for a holy discontent to rise up in people who are sick of bowing down every time anxiety and worry creep up, speaking lies of fear to future situations. Because of this bad habit, too much nonsense is coming out of mouths.

This is the time to not just read about how important our words are or listen to sermons about it. The time has arrived for us to bring life into our world by living it and *speaking it forth with our mouths*. We cannot be satisfied with just thinking about it anymore, because in God's Kingdom, many times nothing happens until we learn to speak and declare it.

It Is Not Just Talk

The Bible tells us in Proverbs that *death and life are in the power of the tongue*. The ramifications of this verse are incredible. They place in our hands the greatest opportunity in this world: to bring atmospheric changes in our world through words of authority and love.

One of my greatest breakthroughs in defeating fear came when I realized that this was not just a pretty metaphorical verse. I took to heart the intense power and responsibility that God had placed in my mouth. I was sobered in humble awe with the awareness that my declarations could literally bring atmospheric changes to my life and the world around me. This revelation caused me to stand a little taller and step up to the divine call of using my words as an execution of God's power and love to this generation. This was more than preaching sermons, because I'd been doing that for years. It pierced me in conviction regarding the very words that came out of my mouth during times of solitude or on occasions where I normally did not think my words mattered. I came to a greater awareness of how I could be a conduit not only for breaking the power of fear, but to undo the works of the enemy in the world.

It is amazing to me how God put so much power in His creation's mouth. Yet with that hefty responsibility is a reality of evil that can be launched with one simple phrase that is spoken. Do not let that fact lead you into fear and condemnation; for from that same mouth, you have been given the power to literally execute life, love and salvation in this world. With the power of the Holy Spirit residing in you, there is a God-given ability for you to change the spiritual climate that you are in, to break the power of fear and cancel the assignment of evil that is on your mind, home and relationships. This is a God-given responsibility that must not be abused, yet at the same time; it cannot be ignored or neglected either.

Watch Your Mouth

James 3:10 tells us that out of the same mouth can come blessings and cursings. Although this should not be, it happens all around us. Why? The reason for this is because there is a spiritual process that takes place when we think on something, believe it and then speak it that brings situations into existence. For example, I could through one sentence or even one word easily cause readers to become hurt, offended or angry, provoking them to close this book and throw it in the trash. On the other hand, I could also with one phrase impart something to the reader that could change their life forever.

While speaking to a crowd, in a few short moments I could cause people to get up and leave the room in disgust. Yet at the same time I can also have the capacity to breathe life into that very same room with words of edification and exhortation spoken from a heart of love. Because of this potency, I am learning each day to listen to what the Father would want me to say, and use my words at a higher dimension for His glory.

While reading this passage in James chapter 3, please realize that the word *curse* is not simply referring to a four-letter word, a swear word or foul language. This is revealing the truth that our words have the power to bring a curse into our lives and into the lives of people around us. At the same time, our words can carry out and impart blessings to those who hear, including ourselves. That shows the power of the tongue.

This revelation must become a sober recognition within us so that we can make covenant decisions with our mouths to be used as vessels of righteousness and blessing. Fear loses its power when it encounters a person who thinks godly thoughts and speaks them. It will usually move on when it sees someone speaking out of an overflow of God's Word that has filled their hearts and minds.

Unfortunately, the influence of society has diluted this principle with the growing use of sarcasm and the popularity of extreme terms that are used to describe everyday occurrences. Sarcasm has made way for people to say things that normally would be unacceptable, because it is now masked in humor. In addition, many excessive expressions are used unnecessarily to add humor to a situation. Yet if continually practiced, these things can have dangerous repercussions.

Certainly we have all made mistakes in this area. How many times do you remember saying phrases like, "I am going to kill him!" or "I'm gonna have a nervous breakdown today!" or even the simple yet ever nagging "What if . . . .?" fear statement.

If we are truly honest with ourselves, there will be a personal realization that much of our talk is fear based. Our thoughts have been fear based and it becomes reflected in our speech. Remember, out of the heart a person speaks. If there is fear in someone's heart, it will eventually come through in their words. But as we pull the reigns on our tongue, there will come noticeable differences in how we talk about our situations and how we even speak to others. It makes room for change and for blessings to flow.

Use Your Rudder

Follow me as I take this thought a step further. Not only is your mouth capable of imparting blessings or cursings, your mouth is also used as a rudder, to bring a course of direction to an entire ship, no matter how large. As you defeat the powers of fear, your plan of action needs to include speaking the Word of God on a daily basis to let yourself and your enemies know your course of action that will not be deterred. Many times it all comes down to your mouth. If you can get a hold and understand the power in your tongue, your whole spirit, soul and body will receive the blessings of it.

In submitting to the will of God in your life, I would encourage you to make it a practice to speak those heavenly things constantly. You of all people need to be reminded of God's purpose in your own life. You cannot rely on someone else to come and speak that for you.

It is your responsibility to steer your course away from fear and into the waters of your destiny. As you approach each day, I would encourage you to take charge of it with your mouth. Most people make the mistake of waiting for the day's thoughts to present themselves, rather than making a firm and godly declaration as to what you plan to think and act on. Make a decision to stand firm with your words, no matter what storms come your way. With that habit in action, you become less of a victim and less vulnerable to fear.

This applies most appropriately to your early waking hours in the day. The spirit of fear loves to take advantage of that weakened state of consciousness where the mind is still foggy and not at full alertness. In that moment of awakening, your mind and body is most likely just coming out of a dreaming brain wave phase as you enter an awakened state. Depending on your sleep patterns, there is a strong possibility there is some sleepy residue hanging until you take your shower or drink a cup of coffee. It is at this stage that the enemy would love to pulverize you with thoughts and impressions that are filled with doom, terror and fret. Many times our spirit can be vulnerable during these tired times because we are not as on guard as we normally would be. That is why many end up having a difficult day fighting anxiety, panic and worry from the moment they woke up. Fear was waiting for them to awaken and did not let them start off on the right foot. Remember, your enemy is not interested in seeing you start off your day strong.

Let me share something that has been helpful to me, because I can be vulnerable in my waking moments. In addition, I am not my strongest in the morning hours. With that in mind, here is some advice. Make a firm and committed decision to start your day thinking and speaking the ways of God to yourself and your situations. Instead of waking up in the morning dwelling and speaking the anxiousness or worries of the day, use your mouth to speak blessings and life into your world. Speak your identity out loud so that it radiates in your spirit and revives your soul so that all of the heavenlies can hear your determination.

The Word of God is your sword, and I would encourage you to start off everyday swinging it by speaking forth the Word of God out loud, before you speak anything else. The day cannot run you over if you have been covered in the anointed Word and by the Holy Spirit who confirms that Word. Be on the offensive with this. Don't just wait until fear arrives. Let your feet hit the ground running spiritually by speaking edification to yourself and to your circumstances with the Word of God. Develop a habit of memorizing certain Scriptures that attack fear, anxiety, stress and worry. Get them into your spirit by speaking them forth until you feel it become a part of your existence. There are multitudes of relevant passages in the Scriptures that deal with all of life's issues, so use it to your advantage.

The devil cannot read your mind, but he certainly can see the thoughts of fear that you have come into agreement with by the manifestations that come through your actions, reactions, and words. Understand that there is an audience in the heavenly realms listening to your words. Satan's desire is to use a spirit of fear to halt your ability to speak what God would have you say. Fear wants to grab your throat and put a choke hold on your ability to speak love, life and liberty to your environment. Breaking fear involves stepping forth and speaking anyway, even when fear is knocking. Both God's Kingdom and the realm of satan's activities are listening to your verbal expressions. Use that power to increase your victory and your territory by speaking the Word of God and the praises of God loud enough so that the devil, the hosts of heaven and all of creation hear it!

Remember, you were called to display the greatness and wisdom of God to all creation, including principalities and powers. Let your words and actions demonstrate it.

To the intent that now unto the principalities and powers in heavenly places might be known by the church the manifold wisdom of God, according to the eternal purpose which he purposed in Christ Jesus our Lord:

Ephesians 3:10-11

Learning How to Talk to Yourself

The great man of God, David, gave us some great examples of the power that can be released through speaking to ourselves. David knew how to encourage himself in the Lord, and through this practice, he would speak in such a way that ushered change into his life and circumstances. Fortunately for us, he recorded them in writing. An example that has really impacted my life is in Psalm 42, where he expresses his passion for God's presence and yet at the same time, recognizes his struggles and hindrances to be free in that. So in blatant honesty, he begins to talk to himself.

Why are you cast down, O my soul? And why are you disquieted within me? Hope in God, for I shall yet praise Him for the help of His countenance.

Psalms 42:5 (NKJV)

He starts off by questioning himself as to the reason for his feelings of heaviness. Yet in response to the question, he does not introspect, neither does he endlessly ponder in search of an answer. His next written thought is a strong message of exhortation to himself: *Hope in God.* There was no explanation or debate. The message was simple. David spoke truth to himself so that his inner man would mobilize and move away from hopelessness and heaviness into a place of hope and rest.

Divine hope is so critical in our lives, and David sought to preserve its value in his life. Even though Hebrews 11:1 would be written much later, David probably knew through experience that hope was a key ingredient for his faith to come forth.[1] When hope is fading or is lost, it can bring devastation and heaviness. Lost hope can even make one sick.[2]

Within this message of hope, David's words encouraged him to step further in praise to God and move away from the position of despair, sorrow and inner chaos[3]. With that posture of praise, he knew that God would help him take back his peace and joy, as he allowed the presence of God to become his primary focus. David was a man who continually allowed his intimacy with the Lord to change his perspective, remove the heaviness and despair, and bring encouragement to his life.

Paul the Apostle not only promoted *speaking* to yourself, he even advocated *singing* to yourself as a way of releasing *personal* and even potentially *corporate* edification. In this, we see the power of praise and worship as an active tool of breakthrough when we cultivate an atmosphere for God's presence to work in our lives.

Speaking to yourselves in psalms and hymns and spiritual songs, singing and making melody in your heart to the Lord;
Ephesians 5:19

The hymns that Paul was speaking of were not *Amazing Grace* or *Come Thou Fount of Every Blessing,* for they would not be written until hundreds of years later. What Paul was encouraging the church to do was develop a habit of using the words in the psalms and in current hymns as spiritual tools for continual edification. The song style or timbre is not relevant, so whatever style of music you prefer is not the issue. What matters spiritually is getting the anointed words of praise, worship and proclamation to become active in your life by speaking and singing them forth. This may be obvious to many, but I must emphasize this: *a practice of praise and worship is an active gesture.* According to scriptural teaching, praise and worship is not just something we just sit and think about—we must step forth and express it. In the context of this passage, it needs to happen verbally through speech and through forming of melody.

This whole topic of praise, worship and the presence of God is a passion for me, and I plan to expand on this in future writings. But when it comes to breaking the power of fear, I ask that you prayerfully commit to speaking and singing the praises of God from your heart as a regular spiritual habit. Even if you find your heart is not engaged, many times it will revive when you make a decision to stand up and walk in a spiritual act of worship unto God.

In the Old Testament, the praises of God were used as weapons. Even choirs were sent out into the battlefields on the frontlines. Many conquests were not even won until the proclamation of the Word of God was sung or shouted.

Even if you do not have a great singing voice, step forward and make melody in your heart unto God. Fill your home with the praise and worship of God. I would even suggest regularly playing music in your home that cultivates an atmosphere of worship and sensitivity to God's presence. This promotes an environment where God is welcome and where fear is *not*. It also helps you to conquer your battles as you sing and proclaim the greatness of God. Praise and worship will remind you of how big God is and how small the devil is. Fear has taught you the other way around, and through seeking God's presence, you will be able to magnify the Lord in your heart while reminding yourself of how awesome He is.

I have found that one of the ways I fight fear, doubt, anxiety and worry is to enter into His presence regularly and let Him fill me with a realization of His character. This has been a true process for me, because I spent most of my life *being afraid* of God, rather than having a biblical awe and respect of Him. Yet the more I am learning that He loves me, the more I sense a deep revelation of the height, depth and breadth of His love and majesty. It changes me inside as I inhale His presence and seek His glory in my life. It takes my eyes off of fear and sets my focus on God's colossal plans for me and His provision that will come along the way. Many times this starts by simply speaking what I know about God and asking Him to further fill me.

If we just sit and think, many times we will get distracted or slip into fearful thinking. The success comes when we speak the Word of God to ourselves and then talk to God out of our identity that His Word teaches. From that place, we allow Him to speak and move divinely in our lives. Most of the time when I feel stuck, I begin to speak and sing the things of God to remind myself of who God is. I make a decision to focus on that while putting a spotlight on all that He has done and will do.

This whole process develops a healthy heart before the Lord along with a sensitivity to hear His voice as we remain aware of His presence at all times. It is out of my heart that words come forth, which shows me that my heart can filled with righteousness or contaminated with all kinds of evil. So guarding my heart leaves a place for God to work, so that words can come forth in purity, love and power.

Thanksgiving

Giving thanks always for all things unto God and the Father in the name of our Lord Jesus Christ.
Ephesians 5:20

Paul continues his exhortation in Ephesians by highlighting the power of gratitude. *A grateful heart fills a person to such an extent that fear has little room to operate, because fear focuses our attention on what we do not have. Thankfulness and gratitude focus on the blessings that have been provided by God; proving that He will surely perform good works in the future.*

This takes away the ability for fear to sting you with dread about the future, because you are so focused on how grateful you are towards God. Cultivating a thankful heart will help you to see that the God who granted you good things in the past will not fail you in the future. Gratitude keeps you steadfast in sustaining a relationship with God that reveals His love, protection and provision; all the blessings that fear tells you will not exist in the future, thus causing more anxiety and worry. Fear will always try to cultivate discontentment.

In order to exemplify this, it is critical to practice this verbally and regularly. I exhort you to let the words of thankfulness and gratitude be an ever present river flowing from your mouth, for it will shower blessings on your life and bring refreshment to dry situations. Fear will cause you to become selfish and focus on all the things you do not have or will not have. Yet a thankful heart is focused on the simple blessings of being alive; like having food on the table and friends to fellowship with. A grateful heart is not focused on future gain or survival, but pursues contentment and thanksgiving, which removes fear's frequency to speak its lies.

Paul even applied this principle of thanksgiving to the prayers that come out of our mouth to combat cares and anxiousness.

Be anxious for nothing, but in everything by prayer and supplication, <u>with thanksgiving</u>, let your requests be made known to God;
Philippians 4:6 (NKJV)

The command is to have anxiousness over *nothing*, but instead in *every* situation and area of your life, develop a spiritual habit of praying from a thankful heart that is grateful for what God has already done. From that vantage point, not only will you chip away at fear, anxiety, stress and worry, but also your prayers will be answered and peace will come to you.

. . . and the peace of God, which surpasses all understanding, will guard your hearts and minds through Christ Jesus.
Philippians 4:7 (NKJV)

With this peace residing in you, there is a spiritual guard set in place, designed to bring protection and safety to your heart and mind. It is not a peace that the world offers, for this world certainly offers a counterfeit peace that is based on the calmness of the situation or on methods of escapism, which can take on many forms. The peace of God is divine and unexplainable by natural means, which is the focus of our next chapter.

---

[1] Hebrews 11:1- *Now faith is the substance of things hoped for, the evidence of things not seen.*
[2] Proverbs 13:12
[3] The word "disquieted" speaks of chaotic, loud, tumultuous, and/or clamorous noise; causing trouble and war within.

Chapter 17

Supernatural Peace:
Take It Back!

For the kingdom of God is not meat and drink; but righteousness, and
peace, and joy in the Holy Ghost.
Romans 14:17

When we sit down and face times of solitude, we discover how much peace we really *do not* have. Because of our fast paced culture, focused on stress-filled lifestyles and speedy deadlines, we are temporarily able to ignore our lack of peace by remaining busy. Yet the relentless schedule and continual movement cannot cover the underlying void within so many that lack supernatural peace. Peace is one of the greatest gifts needed in society today. It is *in* peace that we receive our greatest strength and it is *from* peace that we fulfill our purpose with love and power. It is also a fruit that must not be ignored in the battle against fear.

Paul explained in Romans 14 that the Kingdom of God is *righteousness, peace* and *joy* in the Holy Spirit. I believe there is a divine order to this listing. As the Holy Spirit of God leads us to a saving relationship with Jesus Christ, this opens up an opportunity for us to walk in righteousness (right standing with God) by grace through faith. As a continued progression, the Holy Spirit moves to bring about a work of comfort, healing, deliverance and sanctification in our daily lives. For many believers, a part of this cleansing process involves removing fear. When this is initiated, one of greatest gifts that we can receive begins to manifest in our lives: *divine peace.* One of true marks of a growing believer is the fruit of this peace operating in their life.

When a lifestyle of peace is cultivated, the joy of the Lord has a greater opportunity to manifest itself. But I have often found that *joy has a difficult time being sustained in the life of someone who does not consistently maintain a lifestyle of walking in God's peace.*

For example, try to advise someone who *lacks* peace to consistently engage in expressions of joy, whether it is laughter, dance or exuberant talk. Unless the anointing of God breaks through, you will not usually see long term positive results. If anything, the expressions will be forced and artificial at best. Why? This pattern occurs because *joy usually has room to operate in one who has the freedom of Christ and is walking in peace.* Without that peace, most of the time, there are only temporary spurts of half-hearted elation, leading people to chase after "highs" rather than walking in lasting joyfulness. For those who have battled fear in their life in any form, whether it be phobias, panic, anxiety, worry or stress, one of the greatest gifts of God gets robbed – *supernatural peace.* This must be regained if we are to walk into the promised land of freedom and receive our joy.

The Peace of God vs. The World's Peace

Being a part of the church for over 25 years, I have noticed the astounding lack of peace in too many who are in the body of Christ. Although a significant amount of well intentioned activity and busyness seem to be present, there is an absence of consistent divine peace. This manifests itself in that one of the greatest struggles church people battle with is not being able to be still and spend peaceful time with the Lord. The effects of stress and drivenness push those people to maintain a lifestyle of constant activity that avoids any sign of slowing down and dealing with reality. They usually struggle because there is so much war going on within them. This of course this was not God's original intention.

A large part of gaining that inner peace involves settling quietly before the Lord, turning off the voices and thoughts that seek to clamor for our attention, and developing a sensitivity to the voice of the Father. When fear is removed, gaining a greater ability to walk in divine peace makes room for God's still small voice to be heard.

The world around us is crying, "Peace! Peace!" when there is no peace. Yet the church seems to be suffering from the same predicament. This problem greatly concerns me, because it is out of divine peace that God's people will make Kingdom-minded decisions and reach our world for Christ. *We need that peace so we can give it.* That is why my heart is to see people reconciled to the peace that God wants us *all* to have.

Peace I leave with you, my peace I give unto you: not as the world giveth, give I unto you. Let not your heart be troubled, neither let it be afraid.

John 14:27

There is a peace that Jesus offers His people today. Yet there is also a counterfeit peace that the world offers that is not of God. The peace of the world is built mostly upon fabricated structures of emotional and financial safety as well as habits of running towards various pleasures in order to numb inner pain, fear and brokenness. The divine peace of God is not dependent upon the circumstances of life, nor does it require any man-made device to help in its sustainment. This is a peace that surpasses all understanding and natural thinking. It is also one that must be possessed inwardly, even when situations and storms seem erratic on the outside.

For the church today, true inner peace will be established to a greater degree as the body effectively fights the spiritual war against an enemy that seeks to block rest and peace. Please understand, when believers make committed decisions to walk towards freedom and deliverance, they should expect attacks to be sent to rob them of divine peace. Yet do not be alarmed. We have been given all the weapons of warfare necessary to reclaim the peace that is rightfully ours.

It is also important to remember that true peace will not always fall on our laps. Many times peace needs to be received by stepping out and claiming it. For many, it will involve *reclaiming* that divine peace that has been stolen. Take heart, because Jesus said to be at peace—He has overcome the world! This peace is available to those who walk in the overcoming provision that Christ extends to us. In these days, I truly believe that we are moving into a season where the church will take back the peace that was stolen, and walk in wholeness, allowing the joy and love of the Lord to operate in fullness.

A Storm to Sleep In

In the Gospel of Mark, we find a record of Jesus going out on the ship with His disciples. This account reveals the penetrating power of peace that can come in the midst of a tremendous storm. Most Christians have heard this story through a sermon they have heard, a Sunday school lesson, or a personal Bible study, but it can be very easy to miss the revelation found here if we are not careful.

In Mark 4:35, we get a visual of Jesus commanding the disciples to head to the other side of the sea. On that same day, a few verses earlier, Jesus just finished teaching what the Kingdom of God was like by comparing it to a mustard seed. This mustard seed is a universal symbol of faith that is necessary in the life of a believer if he or she is going to be able to grow and flourish. Little did the disciples know that this was not just a college lecture. This was revelation-teaching combined with immediate application. Their test of faith would take this lesson to a real-life level.

As they begin to make their way out onto the water, a great storm of wind arrives with such punishing effect, that the ship itself becomes filled with water. To the average person, this certainly would create a tremendous opportunity for fear and panic to enter in. But my natural inclination in reading this passage led me to believe that these disciples were mostly trained fisherman who knew the ways of the waters and had experience in how to deal with the storms. With that in mind, their reaction seems a bit strange. It would be like a doctor panicking and not knowing what to do when a patient is brought into his operating room for simple surgery. He does this every day for a living and has years of training.

The disciples were experienced seamen. Yet their condition was no better. The Bible shows us that they were afraid for their lives, which reveals the magnitude of this storm. This was not a minuscule rain storm like they had probably witnessed in previous navigations. This was a weather attack of heavy tonnage. Meanwhile our Savior and Lord is more than quiet, He seems to be in hibernation – sleeping in the back of the ship. This entire vessel is full of water and He is not moving. Jesus is sound asleep! With this entire scenario taking place, the first move the disciples make becomes their first mistake.

Mistake #1
Allowing Fear to Take Over and Become the Leading Motivator

At first glance, most of us could probably sympathize with the disciples for falling into fear. Yet Jesus was calling these fishermen to new levels of authority and faith. His desire was to develop within them a new reaction to storms and attacks. To the disciples, this storm should have been seen as an opportunity for their faith to rise above fear and bring calm to the storm. In addition, Jesus also wanted to train these men to develop a strong spiritual authority over storms by cultivating an inward peace that would overpower them. That godly peace would not be dependent on how serene the waters were, but on how confidently they maintained divine peace within. Instead, in this circumstance, the disciples panicked and feared, which compelled them to run and wake up their Master, who happened to be sound asleep in the back of the ship.

Mistake #2
In Panic, Rushing to Someone to Fix a Storm that God Wants You to Stand Up to Yourself

This leads us to the second mistake, an error that every Christian runs into. *When an attack is brought on us, our instinctive, programmed reaction many times is to quickly call someone on the phone, asking for someone to rescue us out of what we are going through.*

Our Heavenly Father is seeking to teach His people how to stand up to storms and take our rightful authority over the wind and the waves that have come against us. In panic, the disciples asked Jesus to rescue them from the problem that *they* could have taken authority over.

And he was in the hinder part of the ship, asleep on a pillow: and they awake him, and say unto him, Master, carest thou not that we perish?
Mark 4:38

The new contemporary 21st century version of the disciples' plea would sound more like, "Ummm, excuse me . . . . Jesus! Wake up! Do you even care that we are about to die on this ship!? I mean seriously, who sleeps in the middle of a storm?"

In response to this questioning, Jesus reveals the peace that is within Him by acting with such authority and peace. This display would silence the boasts of any brave hero of history. Jesus is not alarmed with fear nor is He even close to panicking. Surprisingly, He does not even acknowledge nor engage the fearful statements of His men. He stands up, ignores the words of doubt and unbelief; walks right past the shouts of fear and goes to work.

And He arose, and rebuked the wind, and said unto the sea, Peace, be still.
And the wind ceased, and there was a great calm.
Mark 4:39

There are many lessons we can gain from this event that would take books and books to cover. But a few spiritual truths stand out in regard to regaining peace when a storm of fear attacks us.

Peace Point #1
Learn to *Not* Engage with the Voices and Thoughts of Fear

Actually, we cannot afford to engage ANY thought that is not of God, but since the subject is fear, I will emphasize that aspect. Too many times our peace is robbed when we attempt to argue with fear. Yet the truth is, fear has not come to argue with you. It has come to bring torment, confusion, panic and insanity. If you try and debate with it and even create a winning argument, fear will find a different crack to sneak into.

Do not debate. You do not need to. Do not try and rationalize with it. Do not even tolerate it. That spirit is not a part of what God sees you to be. His desire for you is to walk in power, love, and a sound mind. Do not allow double-mindedness and condemnation to get you into panic about the decisions you make. Seek the Lord. Seek Godly council from those who are walking the walk that you want to walk. But most of all, make a decision in your heart to push aside what fear presents. Take a stand and speak to the problems at hand with the faith that God has given you. In the process, stand up and take your peace back!

Peace Point #2
There Are Times Where We Need to Stand On Our Own With God and Fight the Storm.

And He said unto them, Why are ye so fearful? How is it that ye have no faith?
Mark 4:40

Jesus rebuked the disciples for the same mistake that we fall into today. Instead of taking care of business themselves, these men gave into fear and ran to Jesus to bail them out. Yet our Savior was seeking to instill in them a confidence and a boldness that would rise up to take authority over the situation and bring about peace in that storm. They had the authority, but they chose not to stand in it.

Next time we are tempted to quickly react and run to someone who we think can fix our problem, it is important to ask ourselves, "Is this a situation that God wants me to stand up to and fight with the authority that He has given me?" Before we entertain thoughts that we have no person to help us and before we think there is no way to find peace, ask, "Could it be that God wants to raise me up as His child to stand in the midst of this storm and bring peace through the power of His Spirit that is within me?" You might be surprised by the answer, because God is training a generation who will answer "yes" to God's call to battle and rise in faith against storms that the enemy brings against us.

There is nothing wrong with receiving help or guidance from a pastor, fellow believer or mentor. I practice and value counsel as a very necessary component in my own walk of faith. Yet along the road, there will be battles that we must face individually in order to go to the next level spiritually. In my ministry experience, I have found that many sincere believers will look to me to remove the bondage or storm that is on their life. Of course I almost always seek to agree in prayer for deliverance. Yet I also strongly encourage believers to take their rightful stand against the enemy themselves. If I can pass on this understanding, then I have not only executed the Kingdom of God, I have also equipped a person for greater spiritual strength.

Learning to stand up to the storms that attack us builds an inner strength and enduring faith in our lives because we have exercised out authority in Christ Jesus. Too many constantly say, "Jesus take it away," where as God may be saying, "I have given you authority to push against that storm. I am on your side and I will be with you. Stand up, speak to that storm and release into the circumstance the peace that I have given you." As believers, God has not only granted us a peace that we can live in daily, He has also given us an authority to speak to the enemy that is attempting to compromise that peace. This leads us to our next area of revelation.

Peace Point #3
There is Often a Spiritual Attack That is Behind the Loss of Peace

Notice the first thing that Jesus did was *not* to speak peace over the waters. He first had to address the storm that was attacking their ship and keeping them from peace. He *rebuked* the storm so that peace would have a place to enter. In the Scriptures, Jesus would repeatedly have to deal with a spiritual issue that was presenting itself as an obstacle to the working of God in a situation. Standing on this ship looking out over the water, I honestly do not think Jesus was simply rebuking the weather. I believe this was a deliberate spiritual attack from the enemy, manifesting in the natural realm to bring destruction upon the disciples and our Lord.

This principle of undoing the works of the enemy *before* releasing the Kingdom of God is all throughout the New Testament scriptures. In the ministry of Jesus, there were times when He would pray for someone and while doing so, would remove an oppressing spirit *before* He would then pray for healing or command a miracle to come forth.[1] Acts tells us that He was anointed by God to heal all those who were oppressed by the devil. With this understanding, we can see that in the spiritual realm, there can be a work of the enemy behind many of our storms, diseases, sicknesses and insanities.

Does this mean that we should look for a demon under every bush and call every problem in our life a result of the devil? Not necessarily, but the church certainly needs to awaken to the reality of a war on the horizon that has been missed, while people have fallen into bondage and oppression. The church must arise and emulate the ministry of Jesus by bringing a full gospel to undo the works of the enemy and extend peace to the nations.

We cannot ignore areas where the enemy has infiltrated any longer. "Out of sight, out of mind" is not a scriptural principle when dealing with satan and his kingdom. Although I do not desire to give him unneeded focus or attention, I certainly do not want to fall into the tragedy of ignoring his work that is keeping lives from freedom. We must not become ignorant of his devices.

Our Lord and Savior lived the example for us, as He came to undo and destroy the works of the devil.

He who sins is of the devil, for the devil has sinned from the beginning. For this purpose the Son of God was manifested, that He might destroy the works of the devil.
1 John 3:8 (NKJV)

The apostles continued in this revelation of authority, deliverance and power in their own scope of ministry. This includes the Apostle Paul, who showed us that we should not focus our main strategic attention on what is happening in the natural realm. Victory takes place when we execute our God given authority in the heavenlies against the storms and attacks that are brought against our peace and destiny.

For we wrestle not against flesh and blood, but against principalities, against powers, against the rulers of the darkness of this world, against spiritual wickedness in high places.
Ephesians 6:12

For the weapons of our warfare are not carnal, but mighty through God to the pulling down of strong holds.
2 Corinthians 10:4

When it comes to your peace, evil spirits of fear, wicked spiritual powers and workers of evil in high places are against you living in that divine blessing. Recognize that the enemy has kept you bound and his influence must be removed for you to begin to take your peace. Stand in your God-given authority as a believer, command that spiritual attack to back off and speak peace where the storm has created torment in your life.

A Peace-Blocker: Unbelief

One of the greatest works of the enemy that can reinforce a spirit of fear and block peace and breakthrough is the spiritual toxin of *unbelief*. It is not only dangerous but also very contagious. Unbelief can be one of the most destructive blocks to seeing a dramatic move of God in our lives.

In our society, there seems to be a prevalent dysfunction that exists which leads people to critically question everything that occurs. Because of this bent towards unbelief, fear has had a more open door to remain. When unbelief is present, faith is not able to operate to its fullest and it causes people to stay heavily focused on the natural realm for hope and security.

Throughout the ministry of Jesus, He practiced the wisdom of staying away from the atmosphere of unbelief. In fact, there were times where He would ask people to leave the room, most likely because of the spiritual atmosphere of unbelief in the room that would come against the healing or miracle. Even though He was the Son of God, Jesus could not even minister in certain areas because of the unbelief that was present.

Going back to the storm that came against the disciples, our Lord basically asked them, "Where is your faith? Why did you fear and begin to lose belief in the power I gave you to rebuke the enemy and speak peace into the situation?" What happened in that boat? Fear and unbelief robbed them of being vessels of miraculous authoritative power.

This truth may shake some people but it can change their walk. Battling fear includes making the decision that we are going to seek God's promises of victory and steer away from doubting His Word and faithfulness. We must learn to lean away from criticizing and negatively analyzing everything that passes before our eyes and instead, look for ways that God *is* working. With this mindset, we will cultivate an optimistic belief in God, ourselves and the people around us. It is with that constant optimism and belief in the delivering power of God that faith, hope and love will be unlocked in our world.

Power Over Storms

Keep in mind that you are fighting an enemy, but it is not your mother-in law, your boss, or your brother in Christ. This is a spiritual power that has to bow to a child of God who is a doer of the Word and walks in the Spirit of Christ. When we begin to recognize who our enemy truly is, we will stop wasting our time arguing with people around us. We will also stop trying to look to all of man's resources to bring healing and freedom to our lives. We serve a God who loves us and is *for* us. He has also given us what we need to be able to stand against the workings of the enemy.

This reminds me of a friend of mine who struggled tremendously with fear, to the point that he was on a number of heavy psychotic drugs to help keep a sense of sanity in his life. He suffered from anxiety, depression and a form of psychosis. My heart always went out to him because I loved him dearly and knew he had a broken heart as I did. Because of this, fear and many other spirits took advantage of him. One night, I got a phone call from him at about 2 am. He called from a local hospital bed because he had a psychotic episode in a local McDonalds and passed out. Because of this, the ambulance had to come and bring him to the emergency room, where he was treated for a massive mental breakdown.

I got a chance to talk with him and we decided to get together the next day. I took a friend with me who was anointed in the ministry of deliverance. We brought this friend of mine to an understanding of what the enemy had done to hold him captive in areas of fear, depression and brokenness. We led him through some brief teaching and then proceeded to pray together. He began to repent before God that he had come into agreement with the enemy in these areas and together, we began to take authority over those spirits. In a matter of hours, I watched this man's countenance begin to clear up and I saw peace begin to come over him as we spoke to those spirits of fear to leave him in the name of Jesus. It was a sight I will never forget. His walk has never been the same again. This moment of ministry gave him a jumpstart into experiencing freedom in his life, and this man is continuing to walk in victory over areas that once paralyzed him. This delivering experience will happen more frequently as believers come into the revelation of who God is and the power they have over the enemy.

As I minister in churches, I am feeling a holy anger at this spirit of fear. God has deeply stirred my heart to lead a warrior's charge of freedom to break fear so that a renewal of God's love and power can take place in the church. Fear had me bound for too long and now it is payback time. With everything that is in me, I cry out to the body of Christ to stand up against the spirit of fear and take your peace back!

Peace Point #4 - Our Goal Should be to Possess a Peace Within that Allows us to Sleep in Storms.

When we decide to come against what is attacking us or keeping us bound in a storm, we also must release what needs to enter—supernatural peace. I have learned when God is bringing deliverance, He not only desires for us to bind what is not of God, but also to release what *is* of Him. When we bind the power of fear and cast it out, we must receive and release the peace of God of which Jesus said He gave us. Yet being given peace is not enough in itself. We have to receive it. Peace is something that must be taken and walked in daily.

In developing spiritual strength, I have found most of the time that I can only have authority over the storms I can sleep in. This is where true Kingdom authority is established in our lives, on earth as it is in heaven. There is no tormenting fear in heaven, so it should not be so in our lives here on earth. It is not God's will for us to be in a state of panic.

In this journey, you must make a commitment to take back your peace. Even if it means you can only hold on to it for a minute, take hold of it; for you will learn to hold it longer, and soon you will hold it for good! It will become a spiritual habit that will follow you in every new adventure. Then you will learn to pull out your pillow in the midst of absolute turmoil and take a nap.

Take It with You

In Matthew 10, Jesus told disciples to bring their peace to the homes they visited. If peace was present there and if peace was received, the disciples were taught to let their peace rest on that house. If peace was not present in the home and the peace that they brought with them was not received, then they were simply instructed to walk out and shake the dust off their feet. I believe that the dust represents anything that the enemy would try to put on you, from strife and offense to fear and worry. Yet this cannot overtake you if you make the decision to hold your peace and rest in it.

This practice of taking, holding and keeping our peace is certainly an active process. It is not something that we should wait for passively. We need to receive it by faith and actively live in that peace. Too many times I observe people just waiting for God to do some magic and put peace on them. They have failed to understand that God works in partnership with our obedience and step of faith to receive and walk in peace.

Receiving peace in our lives also does not mean avoiding all conflict or fleeing from fearful situations. Many run to a sense of peace as their haven, when in reality they may simply be running from a fearful situation they should face. Most likely the things that we are tempted to run *from* are the areas that we need to be running to, so that fear can be faced and defeated. *I have learned that any area where fear contains me is an area where I will be limited spiritually.* In addition, usually the place that fear is attacking is a significant area where God wants to use us mightily in this day and age. Our destiny lies in moving from fear to faith and from panic to peace.

Peace to Hear His Voice

As peace fills us in greater measure, there also comes a better ability for us to hear and know the voice of God, which is one of greatest privileges we have as believers. *Jesus said that His sheep will know His voice.*[2] The problem with those who have battled with major anxiety, worry and phobic issues is that fear took over their thought life and left little room for God to speak. *One of the reasons this happens is because fear has a very loud voice!* In addition, in the midst of this torment, many can confuse the voice of fear as the voice of God, causing a great deal of double mindedness and added confusion. Meanwhile, God is speaking and calling us to Himself in love. His still small voice will not compete with the voices of the enemy. Gaining a greater level of peace also involves sharpening our discernment, so that we begin to know when the enemy is talking and when God Himself is speaking to us.

So how do you hear the voice of God? It starts with removing the voice of fear and learning to know when it is talking. As you tune out fear, you begin to create room for God to speak in divine power. As we remove the work of fear, it is imperative to welcome the voice of the Lord to speak in greater measure.

This also starts with taking your peace on the issues of your life. When I say this, I am not speaking of taking peace with sin. I am talking about taking your peace on the issues that fear will not let you settle on. *If you are in fear or conflict over an issue, take your peace until God shows you what you need to do.* That inner conflict needs to be removed in Jesus name, so that peace can become more active. Once that inner peace is cultivated, especially on a basis of God's love for us, we can create an atmosphere for God to speak.

As a note, be patient with this process. Fear and performance will push you to get it all right today, but God is willing to be patient with you, to teach you how to hear His voice and receive His comfort. Now He does not always speak exactly what we want, *when* we want Him to, but God is looking for us to diligently come before Him and seek Him with passion and determination. For many of you, like me, as God delivers you from the power of fear, you will have a much clearer hard drive for God to write His Word on your life. With that peace, we can experience God's refreshing water of freedom and rest.

---

[1] Luke 13:11-13, Acts 10:38
[2] John 10:27

Chapter 18

Divine Rest:
Run into It

There remains therefore a rest for the people of God.
Hebrews 4:9 (NKJV)

One of the promises available to God's people is the offer for us to continually enter and abide in His rest. As we heed to the voice of God and His peace, we will find His promptings leading us into a greater awareness of His presence and divine rest. It is available to all God's people when they choose to believe Him and enter in. This rest will grant us peace and create an atmosphere in our lives which will act as a force-field of protection against fear, anxiety and stress.

I present this section as an appendix to the previous chapter because it accompanies the arena of peace by teaching us how to enter into divine rest. *Rest* in the Scriptures speaks of the place where we are in total reliance on God's power working within us to establish His Kingdom in our lives. At the same time, divine rest allows us to remain free from *striving*; a way of living that drives us to rely on our own abilities to accomplish supernatural things, yet never produces long term fruit.

I know that many, like me in days past, have searched all over creation, trying to find answers for the issues that were relentlessly distressing and keeping them from peace and rest. Millions have tried all sorts of avenues for help, but found no long term resolution. Divine rest is God's solution for all of His children who will respond to the call and enter in.

Ceasing from Our Own Works

For he that is entered into his rest, he also hath ceased from his own works, as God did from his.

Hebrews 4:10

One of the steps towards peace and freedom from fear involves ceasing from our own works and releasing God to do *His* work in our lives. Unfortunately, this is a completely counter-cultural thought in America and many other regions of the world that have taken on a spirit of self-reliance and drivenness to produce. The enemy has taught many that provision, wealth and success *only* come through burning the candle on both ends by striving to produce until one runs out of gas. Because of this, people continue to press on and labor in their own works, yet eventually end up operating on only fumes and burning out.

On the flip side, God has a Kingdom of paradoxes[1] that teach us otherwise. These seeming contradictions reveal the ways of God's economy that contrast the patterns and methods of our world. For example:

If we want to save our life, we must lose it.

If we desire to live, we have to learn to die (surrender to God and death to the flesh).

If we want to be wise, become a fool.

If we want to be great in the Kingdom, we must be willing to be the least.

In addition to these principles, God reveals that if we are to experience productive success in the Kingdom, it will be found in divine release and rest. Now, I am certainly not advocating as a part of this mindset that we should all sit in a recliner, waiting for provision and success to fall on our laps. What I am speaking of is an activity in the spirit and soul where we are not bound by fear, rejection, performance and drivenness but are led by the Spirit of God in all that we do. This pours out in its greatest power when we learn to daily rest in the Lord.

It must sadden the heart of God to watch His children frantically run around, trying to accomplish great things for the

Kingdom, yet through pathways of striving and performance. Unfortunately, in this fast-paced struggle to survive, God's hands become tied by our unwillingness to let go and surrender our jobs, families, ministries and lives into His hands. The reality is that Father God longs to give us rest while clothing us in His peace and love. All He asks is that we simply *release*.

The power of release in a believer's life was designed to lead them into greater rest. Release seems like a hindrance to achieving success, yet it has a profound effect on the life of a surrendered believer. I have found over the years that the greatest triumphs that came in my life and ministry were in those areas that I released to God by taking my hands off, letting go of control and surrendering the end results to Him. Too often what we end up doing in life is working hard and long all week and then asking God to bless what we did; without first seeking Him and His direction before we did anything. But the pattern gets worse. When we succeed, we continue in the dysfunction, believing the myth that we accomplished everything by *our* own labor. When we fail, we blame God for not coming through. Either way, the bondage to be driven is still there.

In contrast, walking in rest is built on continually seeking the heart of God regarding the situations that we face on a daily basis. In that process, we must release the anxiety and fear that seek to drive us by casting all our cares upon Him, because God cares for us.[2]

Years ago, I met a gentleman whose testimony illustrates the power of release very clearly. His name was Darrel and he grew up in a Christian home with parents who were involved in ministry as pastors. He also had an older brother who followed in his parents footsteps in ministry and became a pastor. As a teenager, Darrel developed a distaste for the things of God and undoubtedly experienced a sense of rejection when his older brother followed after ministry and Darrel did not. As a result, Darrel went into rebellion and walked away from the things of God for over 20 years. His decisions led him into a lifestyle of alcoholism and years of running from God.

During that time, Darrel's mother faithfully prayed and interceded for her son, something any godly parent would do for their children. Every day she would tirelessly lift up petitions to God for her son to come home again to a relationship with God. After decades of frustration and seemingly unanswered prayers, Darrel's mother surrendered her son and released him to God. As he told me the story, this is what I remember him quoting his mom as saying, "God I give my son over to You and I release him into Your hands. He's Yours."

I wish that I had the creativity to make up the end of this story, but I did not, and it is a true story. At the very same time that Darrel's mom released her son, Darrel had his own encounter with God and came to a realization that he needed to leave his destructive lifestyle and come home to Jesus Christ. From that moment on, Darrel has not only been serving the Lord, he has also never turned back to those rebellious and addictive ways. He lives as a testimony of love and grace---but also of the supernatural power of release.

In this journey of ceasing from my own labor I have learned a powerful lesson. *That which I hold on to and keep from completely releasing to the Lord is that which I will probably be responsible for in carrying out the results. Yet that which I faithfully surrender into the hands of God will not only be taken care of, but will bring a compounded return in my life in supernatural ways.*

This applies to every area of your life, including your children, spouse, job, relationships, employees, ministries, bosses, community and church. Release those situations and people to the Lord. Bless them in your prayers and watch God work in mighty power and supply. Release that trying situation that is causing distress in your mind and watch God work in a way you never could have imagined. Release that lost loved one to the Lord and watch God bring them home. Surrender your business fully to Father God and watch opportunities chase you down like wildfire. It is the power of release and surrender! On top of that, you also have the privilege of entering into the promised rest of God, because you have walked in a realm of absolute belief and trust.

Walking in divine rest is not merely a physical action; it is a condition of the heart. In fact, you can be outside chopping wood for hours and be completely at rest. You can be working construction in 100 degree heat and still be at rest within. Why? *Your heart is the place where rest begins.* Out of the heart flow all the issues of life.[3] When your heart is at rest, you make decisions out of peace and faith, relying on God to take care of the results as you obey His direction each day. This is why developing a heart that is tender towards the leading of God is so key to walking in rest. You do as He leads. You speak what He tells you to speak. You move where He tells you to go, like a feather being moved by a steady wind.

Walking in rest is not a list of rules or regulations; it is walking in divine relationship with our Heavenly Father who calls us to rest daily at His feet. As He gives us direction, He will also give us the strength to fulfill it. Flowing by His Spirit should not leave us drained. Being driven to perform or being molded by man's expectations or our own personal fears is completely draining. Striving is fear based; yielding to God's direction is based on His love and provision for those who will trust in Him.

Personal Application

When my wife and I set out to pursue the call that God placed on us which demanded a great deal of faith, we made a very committed decision to always seek what God was doing and jump on that wave. From the beginning, we have sought the Isaac promised direction, not the Ishmael driven direction. So in the beginning we have made some very important decisions that we felt would keep our hearts remaining in His rest. It has been a learning process, but one where God is teaching us to live out His rest on a daily basis.

- When times of crisis or impossibility come, it is fruitless to panic. We have surrendered to God's call and depend on Him. With that in mind, there is a solution and there is provision if we will commit to endure testing seasons and contend for breakthrough.

- The more we rest in His love, the more God gives us divine perspective. We cannot accomplish great eternal matters if we are not continually immersing ourselves in His loving presence.

- As we stay true to our calling, we are going to be free to be ourselves, for that is the most powerful presentation we can give. I am going to be "me" and I refuse to try and copy someone else or attempt to put on a show that is not authentic. I am unique and my greatest effectiveness comes when I can simply speak from my heart filled with love, brokenness and transparency.

- I refuse to make decisions based on fear. Many times when fear is knocking at the door of a ministry opportunity, there is a major breakthrough on the other side. I have watched this happen over and over in my life and in the lives of others. So when I am anxious over a decision, I ask myself, *is this a stage of growth and a new level of trusting God that I have come to?* Many times it is a new threshold of breakthrough that has presented itself, waiting for me to step up and push through.

- I refuse to perform. I minister as myself and then let God show Himself strong. It makes ministry so much more fun and it takes the pressure off of having to have all the answers and putting on a "new show" every time I minister.

- God is in charge of the results. Because I have responded to what I felt He was telling me to do, then *He* is responsible to carry out the results. A loving Father does not abandon His children.

I exhort you to seek the Lord and find out what He has called you to do. Ask God to help you to be secure in who you are. Each of us has something very special to offer the body of Christ at large, and your role is just as important as the next one. Do not let fear and rejection push you into feeling that you have to compete with those around you. If you are not called to be a pastor, please do not try and start a church. You will drain yourself, frustrate the people and in the process, drive your spouse nuts! If God has called you to full time church leadership, stop wasting your time investing your life effort in starting that other venture. He did not call you to do that and it is only going to keep you from His place of rest.

We must all learn to enter into rest by releasing the people and situations around us to God each day. If not, we will be driven to constantly put out fires and take care of every little issue immediately, leading you to an eventual state of burnout.

Come unto me, all ye that labour and are heavy laden, and I will give you rest. Take my yoke upon you, and learn of me; for I am meek and lowly in heart: and ye shall find rest unto your souls. For my yoke is easy, and my burden is light.
Matthew 11:28-30

For all those who are driven by fear to make things happen in their life, take that yoke off and put on the yoke of Christ, for it is so much easier. It is a yoke that is not a binding yoke, but a fulfilling connection with God that ushers in rest. It is better than the heavy load commonly carried by millions.

As a generation, it is time that we turn from the sin of drivenness and performance and move into the rest of God by yoking ourselves with Christ on *His* yoke. The church has tried to get massive results through being motivated by the wrong means. Let's instead, turn it around, run into His rest and watch God perform great wonders in our lives.

Belief Put into Action

Let us therefore be diligent to enter that rest, lest anyone fall according to the same example of disobedience.
Hebrews 4:11 (NKJV)

If there is ever an area where the Bible *does* teach us to be "driven," it is when the Scriptures tell us to be *diligent to enter that rest*. The place where we need a sense of hard laboring is in running daily towards His rest. I know this precept has the potential to overwhelm so many who live in a daily grind of stress and only know to be driven to perform, but it is a Kingdom mind-set that must be established in us if we are to defeat fear and accomplish great things for God. Every morning, when waking up, we are commanded to diligently enter into the rest of God, which will have an effect in every part of our life.

What keeps us from that rest is *unbelief and disobedience*. It prevented the Israelites from seeing the land of promise when they were supposed to and it keeps us today from entering that same spiritual territory. True rest comes to the believer when he or she first believes God's ways. That belief, according to the Scriptures, must be melded with obedient action, revealing our faith and trust in God's provided rest. In other words, I must daily live out my belief that God has rest for me.

When we fail to believe, we miss out on God's rest and we are left to our own frail devices. Because people do not believe in the promise of divine rest, they turn to other avenues for help and other devices to bring relief from their fears and worries. They in fact do not help but lead us into greater bondage. The daily solution comes when we decide to regularly choose to trust God by faith and abide in the realm of rest.

The Bible has no equation for having belief without obedience, so it is necessary for us to act on, by faith, our belief in God's Word and His promises. We cannot wait on the sidelines, but we must step in to this promised rest and seek to abide continually in it.

Obedience is a common thread throughout the Old and New Testament. It is not just an Old Covenant principle. The difference is that the New Covenant makes a provision through the cross and the Holy Spirit to empower believers to obey God and His Word. The Old Covenant was built on fulfilling all the laws, which was impossible to achieve. The New Covenant is built on obeying the command to live in love and to receive by grace through faith the realms of victory and the promises that Jesus lovingly paid for on Calvary. We obey because we have received His love and we live out of that love. We obey because we love Him and *believe* what He says.

And whatsoever we ask, we receive of him, because we keep his commandments, and do those things that are pleasing in his sight. And

this is his commandment, That we should believe on the name of his Son
Jesus Christ, and love one another, as He gave us commandment.
1 John 3:22-23

When it comes to dealing with fear, too many have not come into true obedience to God's Word, and as a result, are struggling with anxiety and worry. It is my conviction that whenever we fall into disobedience, we do so because we have failed to receive the love of God in those areas of our life. God's love has power to set us free and His goodness is what leads us to repentance.

In addition, too many nowadays are trying to bypass their torment and curse by running from God's ways and turning to modern methods. According to these systems, there are many ways that the world attempts to calm the torments of fear, anxiety, worry and stress. Included in this list of modalities are guided imagery, self-hypnosis and yoga.[4] These methods, along with many others are intended to aid people in the lowering of cortisol, the hormone released when fight or flight is in operation. Yet true freedom and rest comes through deliverance and belief that is followed by action.

Our Divine Authority

For the word of God is quick, and powerful, and sharper than any two-edged sword, piercing even to the dividing asunder of soul and spirit, and of the joints and marrow, and is a discerner of the thoughts and intents of the heart. Neither is there any creature that is not manifest in his sight: but all things are naked and opened unto the eyes of him with whom we have to do.
Hebrews 4:12-13

Rest comes as we base our authority on the Word of God as a basis for thinking and acting. Through the power of the Holy Spirit, we must receive revelation from the Scriptures, which will lead us to a place of rest with the Father.

Sadly enough, many folks fail to see God's Word come to pass in their lives and are left struggling to overcome. Yet I do not believe it is God's fault. The problem is on our end. Over the years I have observed that when the Word is not changing us deeply, there are often obstacles that are keeping us from that. Here are examples of possible blocks.

Block #1

The Scriptures have become a religious book that is read to fulfill a ritual, duty, or religious service with little heart and revelation connection.

When this happens, it can be difficult for the Word to have a place to operate in our *hearts*[5] and lead us to life-change. Unfortunately at this stage the comforting voice of the Holy Spirit who leads us in truth is not clearly heard because our hearts are distracted, divided or wounded. The distracted heart needs a realignment of values and treasures, so that it can return to its first love and fall in love with God in renewed passion. The divided heart has to make decisions out a place of complete surrender and trust in God's love and lordship. Yet the wounded heart needs to be touched by the hands of the Master, who loves to embrace His children with restoring love.

This was the mission of Jesus, who said it best when He echoed the prophecy that He came to heal the broken-hearted[6] and bind up those wounds.

The Spirit of the Lord is upon me, because he hath anointed me to preach the gospel to the poor; he hath sent me to heal the brokenhearted, to preach deliverance to the captives, and recovering of sight to the blind, to set at liberty them that are bruised . . .

Luke 4:18

Notice that the Scripture did not say He came to heal the broken "headed". God is interested in healing the brokenness of your heart, because if He has full access to that arena, He can invade every area of your life. If our hearts have difficulty touching Him and receiving His Word, there are most likely areas of brokenness and bondage keeping us from being free to live in His love and freedom. I have witnessed continual ministry opportunities where someone had a tremendous difficulty receiving a breakthrough because they had an incredible difficulty engaging their heart. They would strive and labor to encounter a touch from God and His

Word with little effect, because their hearts were not able to connect. Often they would express tremendous frustration, asking me what to do. God would continually show me that the problem was not the method or the consistency; the root issue was written across their midsection. It said, *Broken Heart.*

With the broken heart lies a dynamic need to experience the love of God in continual fashion. This not only opens up the flow for the Word to come in power, it ushers in a river of intimacy that is revived within the life of a believer. Yet it cannot be done by learning more principles, it comes through *encountering* the grace, mercy, love and forgiveness from Father God.

Block #2
We have not built precept upon precept, but have developed belief systems and doctrines that are not truly based on the totality of the Scriptures.

Too many times we ignore the Scriptures that make us uncomfortable and steer towards the safer verses that "make sense." We are very prone to skip over passages where a donkey delivers a message from God, or where Jesus looks at Peter and says, "Get behind me satan".

In addition, the church has become afraid of certain passages because we are not seeing the same results the Scriptures speak of. Because of this lack of experiencing what the Bible says, we decide to change doctrine rather than change our faulty understanding to make room for the Word to come alive. When we do not see the healings, miracles, or supernatural, we feel the necessity to retreat in our beliefs. This causes churches and fellowships to line up their beliefs with their lack of experience.

For example, God says in His Word that He forgives *all* our iniquities and heals *all* our diseases, but when we do not see it happen, we immediately want to create answers that remove us from responsibility. Instead of regrouping and finding out where we have missed the mark, we change our theology and doctrines to make us feel more comfortable.

I have come to a place of realizing that if the Word is not producing what it says it should, the problem is not God – the growth needs to happen on *my* end! This is not a statement of judgment; it is a statement of truth that God has so much better for us if we will simply contend for it! He is true and faithful and His Word endures forever. So our responsibility is to seek where we err as well as where we need course corrections in our beliefs and let the Word bring renewal in our lives. When this hits home, this is where rest *and* revival come into the picture.

Hebrews 4 says the Word is *quick*; meaning that He has life within Him to "quicken" us. He also has power — effective and active power capable of bringing supernatural change in the life of one that will by faith believe and execute. The Word of God[7] also has the ability to separate the activities of the soul and the spirit of a man, to help bring clarity of truth and to show where the sources of our sinful thought trails lie.

Yet the Word does not end there. It even has an effect that goes beyond the seen world of humanity and has a clear view to the workings of beings that operate on a spiritual plane. The Hebrew writer says that this Word can penetrate the joints and marrow, a very direct physical reference that cannot be overlooked. Can you imagine that the Word of God is so powerful that it can even have a physical impact in the life of the believer to bring that life and power over sin, death and sickness! Interestingly enough, we see a reference to our joints, which help bring structure and allows for movement in our bodies. Even more stunning, the Word can penetrate the marrow, which contains a special life source that is very important to our health: *the immune system.* The Word of God is so powerful, that it can bring alignment to our immune system to keep us in health!

This helps to bring into perspective the passages that Paul wrote to the Romans:

But if the Spirit of him that raised up Jesus from the dead dwell in you, He that raised up Christ from the dead shall also <u>quicken your mortal bodies</u> by His Spirit that dwelleth in you.
Romans 8:11

Unfortunately there is too much in the Word that people are missing out on because they've decided to pick and choose which

Scriptures to take at face value and which to try and change or manipulate. One day on my way home in the car I prayed this prayer, which changed my study and revolutionized my walk with God:

God, I want to be changed to a greater extent than I have ever been. I want to see monumental transformation in my life. So if your Word says it, I want to believe it, act on it and see it reproduced in my life. I choose to not be afraid of what your Word says, because even if you rebuke me, I know you will do it because you love me. My hearts desire is to experience what I am reading in Your Word. So if it's truth from You, I want to live it. Bring it on!

The Word also has an additional effect. Hebrews tells us that there is not a creature that can hide itself from the power of the Word of God. Many think that this means animals or humans. But why would we need the Bible to be able to see things that we can already see with our natural abilities? This leads us to see that there is a supernatural work of satan and his kingdom to bring an attack against what God's Word seeks to accomplish in us. The Word can clearly see demonic activity, which is why we need God to open the eyes of our understanding through His Word.

I am on a quest to bring a revelation to the body of Christ that there is an enemy that needs to be removed from our families, our fellowships and our personal lives. This enemy seeks to kill, destroy and bring torment. The Living Word has the ability to see the creatures that are at work that need to be executed with the Sword of the Word. With this understanding, we can reclaim and possess the peace, health, rest and sanity that God wanted us to have all along.

I believe that God wants to bring a healing to your life that is living, and powerful. I firmly rest in revelation knowledge that God's truth, once it is implanted in your life, can have a massive supernatural affect on you and those around you. You have not even begun to touch the power that God wants to execute through you, and I am praying that this will be a fire to set you free to become all God, your Heavenly Father wants you to be. Let this powerful Word pierce every part of your life. Let it work in its simplest form to bring sanctification to your spirit, soul, and your body.

Rest vs. Performance

I must address this before we move on; because too many times we forget the fact that fear drives, while faith leads. Entering into the house of rest means leaving a performance-driven lifestyle at the door for good. Each morning, we must renew ourselves to be at peace because the Lord is going to take care of us as we cease from our own works, believe and enter into rest. In the meantime, you are going to have to cut yourself slack as to how long it takes you to get there. For so many, you have lived in a performance driven lifestyle to please your dad or your mom and that habit has never left you. Cut yourself a break and allow yourself significant time to heal, grow and walk out of fear. Learn daily to enter into His rest, celebrate the victories and give yourself time to grow in this.

---

[1] Principles that seem to contradict.

[2] 1 Peter 5:7

[3] Proverbs 4:23

[4] http://stress.about.com/od/stresshealth/a/cortisol.htm

[5] The Bible describes the heart as the seat of your passions, treasures, and motivations. It is the place where what you hold dear is located. It is here that we are able to connect through our spirit to God's Holy Spirit. It is also though our hearts that we are able to bring change to bad thought patterns and come to a place of renewing our minds. The Bible teaches that repentance and salvation must start with belief in the heart (Rom. 10:9) and true obedience must come from the heart (Rom. 6:17) or else it is just a religious exercise. True change does not come through just thinking differently, because eventually what is in our hearts will bring out the passionate pursuit of what we really value.

[6] Luke 4:18

[7] Remember that the Word of God is not just a book, but a person – Jesus Christ. The Scriptures are designed to lead us to the Living Word, and it is in that understanding that Hebrews 4:12-13 comes alive.

Chapter 19

The Fear of Man:
A Spirit of Intimidation

The fear of man brings a snare, but whoever trusts in the Lord shall be safe.
Proverbs 29:25 (NKJV)

This section could very well change your life, because the fear of man has no doubt had its effect on so many. Freeing yourself from its grip will in many ways launch you to a new level of freedom that you never knew existed. Yet in fact, most do not even realize they are under its hold. The spirit of intimidation seeks to work in every circle of relationships, from the marketplace to the home and even the church. When this spirit enslaves individuals and groups, people are not free to be themselves and experience joy, peace, love and liberty. Intimidation drives its victims into prisons of fear. Yet worst of all, it keeps the Spirit of God from flowing freely in our fellowships.

By the end of this chapter, I pray that you will develop a higher discernment to identify when this spirit is in operation in people and situations. Breaking its power and walking over its floods of attack will bring greater release to your spiritual walk and raise you to greater authority in the spirit.

Intimidation's Goal

When it comes to breaking the power of fear; especially the fear of man, one of the best passages delivering insight to this issue is found in Paul's letter to Timothy. As a young pastor, Timothy was faced with the daunting challenge of shepherding growing believers in the ways of God; many of whom were elder in years to him. No doubt throughout his ministry encounters, he faced his load of potential fears. With that in mind, Paul gives his spiritual son in the Lord a reminder of what fear is seeking to do in his life by painting a broader spiritual perspective in Timothy's mind.

Therefore I remind you to stir up the gift of God which is in you through the laying on of my hands.
2 Timothy 1:6 (NKJV)

Paul was exhorting his young son in the Lord, Timothy, to minister at his youthful age with boldness and authority. In earlier portions of this chapter he reminds Timothy of his spiritual heritage and also of the faith that resides in him.[1] With that in mind, he also reminds Timothy of the gift of God that is within him through the laying on of Paul's hands.

I am sure there was a special moment that came to Timothy's memory when Paul wrote those anointed exhortations. These written words from Timothy's mentor probably brought him back in his mind to a place of spiritual infilling. It was most likely at the occasion where Paul ministered under the anointing of the Holy Spirit and prayed over this young man and spiritual gifts were stirred up in him. When Paul brought this to remembrance in his letter, no doubt Timothy knew exactly what he was talking about.

Now what is the significance of Paul's charge? One simple reason is because a spiritual gift must be used by a believer or it can lie dormant. Stirring up the gifts is absolutely necessary for the flow of ministry to take place.[2] With this in mind, we have a clearer framework to receive the bigger reason for this exhortation.

What Keeps the Gift of God From Being Stirred Up?

For God hath not given us the spirit of fear; but of power, and of love, and of a sound mind.
2 Timothy 1:7

The context of Paul's message is very simple: ***A spirit of fear's overall objective is to keep the gifts from being stirred up.*** If fear can keep believers like you and me from stirring up our gifts, or if it can convince us that we do not even have gifts, then spiritual ineffectiveness will occur all across the world. Paul told Timothy, *stir up the gift that is in you,* because a spirit of fear is seeking to work against God ordained giftings and assignments. In addition, he needed to know the fear was not from God. Ultimately, when the gift of God becomes stirred up in our lives, fear loses its ability to bring torment because boldness and authority takes over.

The NIV translates the word "fear" in this passage as "timidity," thus adding to our understanding of the word. This word fear speaks of cowardice and remaining in timidity. It can communicate the meaning of being *intimidated.* You could read what Paul is communicating here as saying, "God has not given us the spirit of *intimidation.*" Intimidation, or the fear of man, will seek every opportunity to keep you from truly knowing who you are in Christ and prevent you from stepping out in boldness to minister the love and power of God.

Signs of Intimidation

In the body of Christ, intimidation or the fear of man[3] attempts to work in every aspect of church life; seeking to keep the gifts from operating fully. It can be a very subtle spirit and will attempt to covertly keep people from stepping out in faith and boldness. Intimidation can drive pastors to shrink from strong confrontations because of the politics within their church, often stemming from the position people hold or the amount of money they give. Church boards can often crush their pastor's gifts and potential with a spirit of intimidation, causing them to lose their ability to lead with authority, security and boldness.

For many in the church who are affected by this spirit, everything can seem nice until people do not get what they want. It is at this point that true motives reveal themselves and power struggles can begin to surface. Often times, when intimidation is at work, people will use money, position, Bible knowledge, spiritual experience and countless other tools to bring leverage against others. Freedom and liberty become locked up, and love is counterfeited and conditional. Meanwhile the sense of God's fresh presence becomes distant. Many leaders use intimidation against people in the church, but it can also be used by members in the body who seek to drive their own personal agendas and leadership ambitions.[4]

The Trap

The fear of man brings a snare, But whoever trusts in the Lord shall be safe.

Proverbs 29:25 (NKJV)

The word "snare" in the Hebrew is the word *môqēsh*, which describes a noose for catching animals. The definition of this word also implies a hook for the nose that leads you to that snare. This snare becomes the prison where a person affected by it becomes trapped.

The illustrated meaning here is that being intimidated by other people has a lure which will lead into a stronghold of bondage. Yet this message is not just for those who are *being* intimidated. The one *using* intimidation against others is in the snare as well. They are just as trapped, if not more so. The reason is that people who use intimidation as a tool often do not realize that they are under the clutches of the very same force (fear) in their attempts to obtain and maintain control. Most "intimidators" saw it as a method of motivation they watched others use. Intimidation can also be a quicker and easier way to bring others into submission, rather than lovingly and patiently guiding them towards their best future; not just for one's own personal campaign.

Most people who use intimidation are very insecure inside. They are threatened when others around them begin to grow in authority or influence. They also do not like to see other people shine brighter or come up with creative ideas that are better than their own. Because of this insecurity, fear comes in and programs them to take *control*. When control enters, this is when manipulation and witchcraft come into operation.

Witchcraft

When most people think of witchcraft, they have a mental image of someone casting spells, doing a séance, or conjuring up evil spirits. But this is not the sole definition of witchcraft. Certainly occultism has aspects of witchcraft in it, but the kind of witchcraft I speak of has to do with *control* and *manipulation*. These two work together, driving people to attempt to take over situations through ungodly means. This maneuvers people and circumstances towards a specific agenda. The inherent danger with control and manipulation is that the hand of God does not have the opportunity to move freely and bring liberty to His people. Unfortunately the world *and* the church are full of this poison. Yet in order to completely defeat it, the battle must be fought spiritually.

Control, a major component of witchcraft, can slide in easily when people push their agenda in a way that must line up only with *their* ideals. Control is the opposite of release and freedom. Those who have this spirit seem to always be around, attempting to push their campaign and bring an emphasis to their agenda. They have a tendency to listen to what is happening, not to be a help, but to influence anywhere they can to keep control. Leaders who operate in control only let people grow when it happens according to *their* structure. Having unique ideas or opinions on issues is often not allowed. Under this mindset, freedom is only allowed under the careful watch and oversight of the *one* in charge. Every move that people make in the organization is monitored. When anyone steps "out of line" the hammer comes down to put people in their place. Unfortunately in the church, control affects both pastors and church members. Those who are in church leadership need to repent of this and allow God to move through the lives of the people. Those in the church need to repent for giving in to control and need to humbly submit to God and the leadership He has established.

Manipulation reinforces intimidation by working any angle to get a desired goal in place. It is not of God and produces an oppressing spirit of fear and witchcraft in the church that gives no room for the Holy Spirit to sovereignly move in the hearts of people. Those who manipulate usually end up getting involved in gossip and play both ends of conversations to gain an upper hand. One moment they speak highly of you, the next moment they become an adversary. Confusion enters because you never know where people stand. Meanwhile, no one is free to live and move in love and safety. Can you see why this is such a trap?!

To get a framework of manipulation, control and intimidation from the Scriptures, 1 Kings contains a dynamic example. The prophet Elijah came under the influence of this spirit of witchcraft and intimidation. Interestingly enough, it occurred right after he witnessed a mind-blowing miracle on Mount Carmel before the prophets of Baal. Jezebel, the biblical example of intimidation and witchcraft, finds out that her prophets were embarrassingly defeated at this spiritual showdown. In reaction to this loss and the killing of her prophets, she retaliated with a harsh message of fear to Elijah.

Then Jezebel sent a messenger to Elijah, saying, "So let the gods do to me, and more also, if I do not make your life as the life of one of them by tomorrow about this time." And when he saw that, he arose and ran for his life, and went to Beersheba, which belongs to Judah, and left his servant there.
1 Kings 19:2-3 (NKJV)

You would think that an anointed man of God like Elijah would think nothing of a threat like the one from Jezebel; especially after all that God did in his life. Yet instead of Elijah remaining calm and confident in the Lord, he panicked under these words of intimidation and ran for his life. In a moment, he completely forgot about the victory on Mount Carmel and escaped in panic, which led him to later feeling afraid, isolated and depressed.

The truth is, when Elijah came under this spirit of intimidation and witchcraft, he lost his vision and spiritual authority. In fact, if you continue reading the account in 1 Kings, not even the presence of God visiting him could help him climb out of his depression! This is why we need to open our eyes of discernment to recognize when these tactics of the devil are manifesting in our circles of relationship. If we fail to do this, our relationships can become "side winded" by the enemy's attacks.

Intimidation's Other Friends

When the fear of man is in operation, there are added tools that join in to reinforce and keep people locked into intimidation. When normal motivational techniques are not working, many times people will give in to *anger* to push people into their place. Although there is such a thing as righteous anger (as in the example of Jesus flipping the tables) too many times the expression comes forth as destructive wrath, through harsh words or violence. When this manifests, people who become intimidated end up panicking and retreating in fear. When you come right down to it, this is basically the bullying technique: *get people to retreat and submit to you by using threats and controlling tactics.*

Although I do not have time to cover these next add-ons to intimidation in great detail, the **Leaven of the Pharisees** and the **Leaven of Herod** will certainly contribute to this fear of man that seems to plague many fellowships. The Leaven of the Pharisees is defined by a mentality that confines God and His ways into a box that is mostly man-made, with traditions and rituals that often become valued higher than what God sees as important. This religious spirit always attempts to keep things the way they are and to see God move only in a certain way that a group deems acceptable. Now the Bible certainly teaches that church leadership exists to keep wolves out and to guide the people, but too often it has turned into a stale and cold religious model that lacks the power of God.

The Leaven of Herod partners with the Pharisees because it is a political spirit. Its main emphasis is on being involved in political struggles and strategizing in the affairs of decision making and policy. The Leaven of Herod is always concerned about what people think and places the opinions of the people higher than God's direction. It is very easy to see why this spirit is akin to the Leaven of the Pharisees and a spirit of intimidation.

Victory Over the Fear of Man

Removing the fear of man or a spirit of intimidation must be done through repentance from it and through standing in our spiritual authority. Healing needs to take place in our relationships and fellowships for the effects of this dysfunction to cease. This turnaround will also require a renewal in our hearts, leading us to deeply know that we do not need to fear *any* man.

As we recognize where we have come under intimidation; whether it be at work or at church, we need to understand that breaking the fear of man occurs at a greater level when we repent for idolizing what people think above what God says. Anytime we value the opinion of man above what God says about us, we will find ourselves in place of being victim to what others think and say about us. The ideal place is to seek for approval and personal validation from Father God Himself before we ever look to man and his opinion. It is easier said than done, that is why I am such a firm believer that we need a daily experience with God's love so that we can be secure in who we are in every interaction!

As an added exhortation, let me remind you of Jesus' words in the book of Matthew:

For whosoever will save his life shall lose it: and whosoever will lose his life for my sake shall find it. For what is a man profited, if he shall gain the whole world, and lose his own soul? or what shall a man give in exchange for his soul?

Matthew 16:25-26 (KJV)

As I look over this passage, I am reminded that in my own walk and in the lives of many others, we are always looking to *preserve* ourselves in situations. When it comes to dealing with fear, we become vulnerable because we are so deeply concerned with self-preservation: maintaining our image and position in this world. This mindset leads us to ask the question, "How does this affect *me*?" in every circumstance.

In breaking the power of fear, if our desire is focused on saving our lives in our own strength and resources, we will always be vulnerable to fear, because we have not fully released ourselves into God's hands. We are way too concerned about preserving our reputations and our security. Jesus tells us to lose it, so we can find it.[5] The transformation comes through giving Him full ownership of our hearts and identities.

If we humbly "lose our lives," over to God, it is then that we will truly find *who* we are and *what* we were meant to do. It will position us to surrender all for the sake of following God's call. It also burns out the vulnerability of being so deeply concerned about what people will think of us.

Stop Caring?

Ultimately, fear has no place in someone who does not care what people think. I know this can be so much easier said than done, but it is truly the point at which fear has no entrance. A heart that truly believes *only* what God thinks about them is the heart that will not fail because of fear. This does not in any way imply an attitude of disrespect towards people; it is an issue of being firmly established in what God says about us. With this revelation, we become less vulnerable to the fear of what others can say or do to us.

The LORD is on my side; I will not fear: what can man do unto me?
Psalms 118:6 (KJV)

Sometimes I will scream this at the top of my voice until it resonates in me and becomes a part of my identity. Honestly, if the Lord is on our side, what in the world can man do to us? What is the worst thing in the world that could happen to you; you die and go to heaven? I know that sounds facetious, but it is foundationally true. Our God has our backs. What can anyone really do to us that is worth seeing as a threat? The honest answer is *nothing*.

Overcoming intimidation involves being sure in my identity in Christ. Having triumph over fear comes in knowing that God has my back and will always take care of me. I can know that no man is my provider. No person in this world is my source. My Daddy in heaven is my supplier, provider and He is my source. With that in mind, I need to be more concerned about what *He* thinks than what any person thinks of me.

Overcoming the fear of man happens when I truly get immersed in the love of God, for it will revolutionize every atmosphere in my life. Love has the power to change relationships and the way we see people. Love is the paramount thing when it comes to the Kingdom of God. It has power to blast out sin, change lives and usher in the freeing, delivering power of God. People will follow you in greater freedom when your love for them is your highest priority. You will also see people changed to a greater degree and the power of God will manifest more when love is cultivated in a fellowship.

I have to be honest with you. I cannot minister to you in my full capacity if I am afraid of you. In addition, I cannot love you if I am afraid of you. I also will not be able to lead you or challenge you if I am also afraid of you. This fear needs to be removed and love needs to come in so that God's people can live in freedom.

I cannot stress this enough, because it has become my life message: perfect love casts out fear and love is above all things. When you experience the love of Father God on a regular basis, you will have much less of a tendency to search for love and acceptance in people. In fact, it will make you more secure when you *are* with others, because you will not be starving for them to fill you.

The love of God is the most powerful thing I have ever experienced in my life. It has changed what could not be changed in my life. True love has allowed me to minister to people in divine power because I was first moved with love. Love is a matter of the heart and cannot be faked, but when it comes, there is no power like it.

---

[1] I find it very fascinating that in the description of Timothy's heritage, you hear about his mother and grandmother's faith, but nothing about his father. This rarely every occurred in the recording of Scripture. Usually the lineages were described through the line of the fathers. This leads us to ask, "Where is Timothy's father?" It also shows us why Timothy probably had some vulnerability to fear (a topic that Paul addresses with him), because of his lack of a father. It also shows the blessing of Paul taking the place as a spiritual father in his life—a much needed paradigm in the church today.

[2] Some translations say to "fan the flame" or "kindle afresh" the gift.

[3] I will use the fear of man and intimidation interchangeably because I believe them to mean the same thing.

[4] My emphasis is on the church being freed from this spirit of intimidation, but it certainly needs to fought against in every mountain of society, including business, family, politics and finance.

[5] Matthew 16:25

Chapter 20

Those Who Have Gone Before Us

Therefore we also, since we are surrounded by so great a cloud of witnesses, let us lay aside every weight, and the sin which so easily ensnares us, and let us run with endurance the race that is set before us.
Hebrews 12:1 (NKJV)

Hebrews brings a reminder of people who have gone before us and have stepped out in faith to accomplish amazing things for God. They were instilled with a hope that pointed to a promise that was *yet* to come. With that hope, faith had an opportunity to work, because faith brings substance to that hope. These godly men and women executed faith in such a way that it brought a walk into their *daily* existence that anticipated the fulfillment of that promise. Across the ages, men and women of God have been able to do great exploits and accomplish wonders for God by faith. Yet at the same time, tremendous obstacles of fear stood as road blocks to the achievement of their assured destiny. Some overcame fear, while for others, fear became their downfall. What sets people of faith apart from others has been their determination to obey God and walk by faith, which usually leads them to face fear in many forms.

Hebrews 11 gives many examples of people of faith and I am sure we could make a list of thousands of others that could be added to that list. Yet what we see in Hebrews 12 is astounding, because the writer tells us that there is a cloud of these who are called *witnesses,* who are watching and cheering us on to see the completion of that which they so faithfully began. They now surround us in the spirit, applauding our every response to break fear and walk in faith. Interestingly, Hebrews tells us that these men and women of faith *need* us, because without our steps of faith, they will not be made perfect. They are watching us today to see the completion of what many of them began and what they all gave their lives for! They are cheering and supporting our walk of faith. I pray that by the power of the Holy Spirit, the veil will be pulled back and you will see the inheritance they left behind for you to take and bring to the next level by faith.

In this chapter, I want to bring an exhortation to you by revealing people in the Scriptures who had to face the onslaughts of fear. It is their examples that we must use to bring life and victory to our circumstances so we can overcome fear and accomplish what God calls us to *be* and *do*. These can be tremendous passages of Bible study to bring revelation and breakthrough.

Abraham
Genesis 12-20, Romans 4, Hebrews 11:8-19, James 2:21-23

We fittingly begin with Abraham; the man who was promised that out of his seed would come a great name and a great nation of inheritance and blessing. This process began when Abraham (at that time he was Abram) heard the Word of the Lord and stepped out in obedience. This move of faith was unquestionably intense, for it required Abraham to leave his country, his father's home and his people to step out, not knowing where he was going.

For those who step out in radical obedience, fear will come in its strongest fury to completely wipe out our stamina and faith. Yet it is faith that pleases God and pushes back fear.

The level of risk usually corresponds with the level of faith that is built into us as we hear the word of the Lord and step out, trusting that He will meet us all along the way. Abraham's radical obedience was not only met by God, but the promise that began with Abraham sent forth a spiritual legacy that is still in operation today by faith. Abraham's message to those who face fear I believe would be this: *Stepping out in radical obedience by faith will bring an inheritance for generations to come!*

Yet before you become overwhelmed with stories of greatness, recognize that Abraham certainly had shortcomings along the way as He walked with God. His promise, given by the Lord was laid in the fact that there would be a child coming from his seed and the womb of his wife Sarah. Yet they were both old in age and way past the usual time of giving birth. Yet as God brings this promise, he reminds Abraham not to give in to fear.

After these things the word of the LORD came unto Abram in a vision, saying, <u>Fear not</u>, Abram: I am thy shield, and thy exceeding great reward.
Genesis 15:1

Initially, Abraham believed, but would later struggle with fear and impatience because the promise did not come in the time that he estimated in his natural thinking. Motivated by this fear, Abraham is driven to have a child with Hagar, Sarah's handmaiden, who was named Ishmael. Yet this child was not the fulfillment of the promise. Isaac, born of Sarah would be the child that brought forth the promise of God.

Do you ever notice that fear always seems to point to the areas where God has not shown up yet? Meanwhile, God is at work behind the scenes, orchestrating in the heavenlies a work that cannot be fabricated with human hands. As you believe and trust Him by faith with patience, not only will you overcome your fears, you will walk into greater lands of promise than you ever knew existed! My encouragement to you through the lesson of Abraham is this: *always look for the Isaac in your life.* Do not ever let fear cause you to settle for Ishmael.

Abraham also struggled with the fear of losing his life and with the fear of man when he lied *twice,* both in Egypt and in Gerar. His deception came out when he said his wife was his sister. When push came to shove, his thoughts were not to protect his own wife; his concerns were focused on the fear of losing his own life. So we see clearly that even though Abraham was a man of great faith, he still had major struggles with fear and other sins. This should bring great encouragement for you to know that failure is not the end. You can still stand up today and plow through the spirit of fear and walk into your land of promise. His grace is still sufficient to lead you to victory.

Moses
Exodus 3-4, Hebrews 11:23-29

We can learn great lessons about fear from Moses because he struggled with the fear of man. In Exodus 3, God appears to him in the burning bush and begins to reveal His divine nature as well as His plan for Moses. Even though Moses has a massive encounter with the Lord, there was still a stronghold of fear on his life, as we can see in his reaction to the calling. As God reveals His plan of deliverance, Moses was intimidated at first because he struggled with a slow and stuttering tongue, which in his mind eliminated him from being able to minister and lead. Yet in God's Kingdom, our Father in heaven does not focus on our shortcomings. He sees our divine nature that He created and He works to see the potential for that divine life to spring forth.

The fear of man (the spirit of intimidation) can produce stuttering and a difficulty to speak confidently. I have witnessed it in operation where one becomes locked in shyness and passivity because of it. For Moses, it was a hindrance that needed to be broken. It also needs to be shattered today if this generation is to speak the word of the Lord with boldness. Just like Moses, you too can overcome this fear of people and intimidation by receiving revelation from God's Word and power from the Holy Spirit. In addition, through "burning bush-like" encounters with God's awesome presence, you can take your faith to the next level.

God in his mercy temporarily pacifies Moses' words of fear and doubt by allowing Aaron, his brother and the first high priest of Israel, to be his godly spokesperson. When fear is at the helm in our lives, we will develop a familiar tendency to gravitate towards keeping something familiar as a backup in case things go wrong. The problem is, you cannot run to second base while keeping your foot on first. You cannot sail into the sea towards new land while sailing close to the shore that you left from. Moses looked to Aaron as the man that he could hide behind.

How many times does this temptation rise up in us? We sense that God wants to use us to march forward in boldness to a new territory. Maybe it's a new job, a new sermon, a new ministry, a new relationship or an act of boldness that requires great strength.

The lure that fear brings at those crossroads is to get you to hide behind a standby in the natural to give you support, when God is seeking for you to let go of the supports that you always relied on and surrender yourself into His love and care. Fear will tell you that God will not help in that moment when your foot steps out. It will get you to run to natural man's resources for your protection. Fear will cause you to develop all kinds of backups from friends, leaders and bank accounts. Faith says that God will not only meet you at that step, but He will walk with you through the journey with guidance and provision.

Moses started off by looking to Aaron as his lean-to. Yet when the moment of truth appeared, you see a totally different Moses. When he stands before Pharaoh at the time to declare the Word of the Lord, you do not see Aaron speaking forth for Moses. You see Moses stepping forward and walking in his authority. I wonder if Aaron looked over in amazement when this happened!

What happened? Moses realized that his fears were all smoke, mirrors and illusions. There was nothing to be afraid of. When Moses would speak, God was going to be with him through it all to deliver him and the people. In fact, Moses did not need to rely on his brother to be the mouth piece of Israel when God called Moses himself to be the messenger and leader. Moses' message to you today as he cheers you on could be: *Step out in faith. Exercise your calling and gifting and see the hand of God work in power.*

Shadrach, Meshach and Abednego
Daniel 3

The account of these three Hebrew men is a classic exhortation in facing fear and intimidation. Their example has humbled me and deeply challenged me to seek for a greater level of inner boldness to stand for God in power. Their example would make the strongest men of battle cringe.

These three men were pulled out of the group of captured Hebrews to serve in the Babylonian kingdom. In a context of serving under an ungodly empire, God honored their integrity and faith and granted them favor before the king's leadership. They could have easily ridden the coat tails of their favor to pursue pleasure because of their esteemed status. Yet their number one concern was to honor God and keep His ways alive in their hearts.

The turning point of contention arrived when king Nebuchadnezzar built a statue designed as an object for people to bow down to and worship. On a special designated day, the music played and the command was given for all people to bow down and worship this graven image. For most Christians today, it would be a convenient opportunity to bend over and tie your shoes, as an excuse to avoid any pending punishment in the fire filled furnace. Yet their decision was to stand tall in honor of Who was truly the King – the Lord God Most High. With this tremendous step of faith and boldness, Shadrach, Meshach and Abednego reveal to us a very important principle: *the fear of the Lord defeats the spirit of fear, because God's power and presence cannot be matched by the enemy.* These men had such a deep revelation of God's awesome nature that their words to the king after being arrested for disobedience were astounding.

Shadrach, Meshach, and Abednego, answered and said to the king, O Nebuchadnezzar, we are not careful to answer thee in this matter. If it be so, our God whom we serve is able to deliver us from the burning fiery furnace, and he will deliver us out of thine hand, O king. But if not, be it known unto thee, O king, that we will not serve thy gods, nor worship the golden image which thou hast set up.
Daniel 3:16-18

The power of this statement cannot be communicated in words alone. They were so committed to obeying God that even if He let them down and allowed them to be burned, they were not going to be offended with Him, nor were they going to retreat from their stand. That is the kind of revelatory power that needs to operate in this generation.

Simply put, they feared the Lord more than they feared man. Even if God let them die in the fire, they were not going to bow. They respected the king's authority and they honored his every request, until he asked them to disobey God's commands.

Imagine what would happen if you applied this principle to your marketplace work. What would happen if you honored your bosses instead of gossiping about them, and yet at the same time, refused to engage in dishonest business practices with them?

The lessons from this account in Daniel are endless, but I desire to see it light a fire in your life to help you overcome fear. Their message to all of us today could quite possibly be this: *Cultivate an awe, reverence and godly fear of the Lord that overshadows the tormenting fear of anything else.*

Gideon
Judges 6-8

Gideon was certainly in no place to receive what was coming to him. An angel appeared and sat under a tree to deliver a message from the Lord to Gideon. The message was a powerful one: *God is with you, you mighty man of valour.* This declaration should have given Gideon strength and vision, but the problem was that he was insecure and full of fear. This is an encounter that most people would give anything to experience, yet he responds as though the angel was speaking about someone else. Yet despite these inadequacies, God called Gideon forth by speaking to him not as he *was*, but as he would *become*, a man of bravery and courage. His name meant "he who casts down" and that is what God was seeking to pull forth in Gideon.

Even though Gideon was full of fear and doubt, he stepped forward in response to the call and God used him mightily to bring triumph. He took a mere 300 men and brought panic and destruction upon the Midian army and watched and as their enemy fought and killed each other. Because of Gideon's great exploits, the land was at peace for forty years and he finished his life out in honor. I believe his message to you regarding dealing with fear could be: *When God is with you, it pays to face your fears and do battle with your enemy.*

Jeremiah
Jeremiah 1

There are very few people who have had a tougher job than this man. Known as the "weeping prophet," Jeremiah was called to preach a message of repentance and call the people of Israel away from sin and back to God. Through this time of prophetic ministry which would last for decades, he would witness the invasion of the Babylonian armies, the deportations and killing of God's people and the destruction of the temple. He would later mourn and lament over Jerusalem, knowing that the people did not listen to the warnings. Yet he fulfilled his mission and calling by proclaiming that word and walking in boldness.

Yet God had to show him as a young man to be confident in his identity and calling. The Lord knew this young prophet, who was probably a teenager at the time, would have to overcome tremendous fear in order to minister with authority. God commanded Jeremiah to not see his age as a boundary to his destiny, for the Lord called him from birth to be a prophet unto the nations. In addition, the fear of rejection needed to be attacked if he was to speak the Word of God to people who would not receive it.

Be not afraid of their faces: for I am with thee to deliver thee, saith the LORD.
Jeremiah 1:8

Jeremiah's message to those who battle with fear would probably be pretty straight forward: **Do not allow the fear of rejection or the fear of man to keep you from speaking the word of the Lord with boldness!**

Jesus Christ
The Gospels

I cannot bring examples from the Scriptures regarding overcoming fear without emphasizing the example of Jesus. His *life* is the greatest example. He lived in constant communion with the Father and lived a life void of stress, anxiety or worry. He knew when to get away and he knew when to say "no." He knew when it was time to minister to the masses and when it was time to be with His disciples. He demonstrated a perfect balance of life which gave Him tremendous authority over fear. During His years of ministry, he taught a great deal on how to live a stress free life.

In Matthew 6:34, Jesus said "Therefore do not worry about tomorrow, for tomorrow will worry about its own things. Sufficient for the day *is* its own trouble." His command to "not worry" gives us the opportunity to walk in power, love and a sound mind each day. In the morning, you can wake up; take tomorrow's worries and put them aside. That way you can do what God created you to do: enjoy, serve, play, work and live in the here and now. Too many have been robbed of the joy found in today because they are obsessed with worry about tomorrow. In the meantime life keeps passing them by.

There is certainly nothing wrong with planning or with long-range goals, but my question to you is, "What is the spirit behind it?" Are you planning to make sure that every little detail is covered so you can worry less, or are you planning, leaving large gaps that God will have to fill in because you have given Him as much room as He wants to work?

I can hear people saying, "Mark is it that simple? I'm just going to simply step out in faith, not worry and lay my head to bed at night knowing that everything is going to be ok?" I am with you and I understand that this can be a challenge. But I am finding out that the more I step out in that kind of faith, God honors His word and works in power to release a greater sense of peace to sleep, rest and enjoy life to the fullest. I find that as I arrive at the edge of my "decision cliffs" and step out, I am learning to believe that He is going to catch me, no matter what. I have to believe that or else I will never take a risk or try something new. Each time as I take that step out, I get tempted to think He's going to drop me. Just as I feel I am going to drop, He catches that next step. The great thing is that He walks me through *every* step.

This does not mean that I still do not battle with worry, anxiety, doubt and unbelief. I still have battles to overcome. But as I continue forward in faith, there becomes less and less room for that junk to work. In fact it begins to dissipate in the face of living and active faith.

The Early Apostles

But ye shall receive power, after that the Holy Ghost is come upon you:
and ye shall be witnesses unto me both in Jerusalem, and in all Judaea, and
in Samaria, and unto the uttermost part of the earth.

Acts 1:8

The men who were sent by God with the gospel certainly had to face their share of fear-attacks. Yet they were called to be spiritual pioneers who would establish a work of God and lay out a foundation for the church to live by. On the day of Pentecost, this new baptism of the Holy Spirit ushered in a new power and endued upon them an anointing that allowed these ministers of the Lord to infiltrate their society with divine power. In the passage above, the word "witness" actually means *martyr,* or *someone who gives their life for the cause.* In this case, Jesus was telling His followers that they would receive power and boldness to the point that they would be willing to die for the sake of the Gospel. It seems almost unimaginable, but this group of unlearned individuals ended up turning their world upside down as a radical explosion of the Holy Spirit moved upon their lives.

These men lived in great faith by grace, and they refused to allow the fear of man, fear of death or the fear of rejection to bind them from their divine mission. In multiple cases, these men ended up giving their literal lives for the cause of the Gospel of Jesus Christ. Their martyrdom is recorded effectively in *Fox's Book of Martyrs: A History of the Lives, Sufferings, and Deaths of the Early Christian and Protestant Martyrs.*[1] Much of what follows is taken from that book and reveals the intense dedication to the death that they possessed. Let it build your faith and edify your spirit to rise up in greater boldness.

Stephen - Stephen was a man of faith, full of the Holy Spirit who ended up being cast out of the city and stoned to death.

James - James the son of Zebedee, the elder brother of John, and a relative of Jesus; for his mother Salome was a cousin to Mary, was beheaded along with another.

Philip – Philip was martyred when he was scourged, thrown into prison, and later crucified.

Matthew - Matthew wrote the gospel that bears his name and suffered martyrdom by being slain with a halberd.

James - He was elected to the oversight of churches in Jerusalem and also wrote the Epistle that bears his name. At the age of ninety-four, he was beaten and stoned by the Jews.

Matthias – Elected to fill the vacant place of Judas, Matthias was stoned and beheaded at Jerusalem.

Andrew – As the brother of Peter, Andrew preached the gospel to many nations, but was taken in Edessa and crucified on a cross.

Mark – It is said that Mark was converted by Peter, whom he served as an amanuensis (a Latin word used to describe someone who by hand, writes down the words of another). It was attributed that Mark wrote the gospel named after him under the examination of Peter himself. At the hands of the people of Alexandria, Mark died terribly by being dragged to pieces.

Peter – Peter, the one who made plenty of blunders while Jesus was in ministry, experienced dramatic growth along his journey. When he was filled with the Holy Spirit, we saw a new man step forward in boldness, preaching the gospel and doing signs and wonders all throughout the world. His death would show us his extreme passion and faith to the gospel of Jesus Christ. The best way to show this is to quote from Fox's Book of Martyrs.

> *Among many other saints, the blessed apostle Peter was condemned to death, and crucified, as some do write, at Rome; albeit some others, and not without cause, do doubt thereof. Hegesippus saith that Nero sought matter against Peter to put him to death; which, when the people perceived, they entreated Peter with much ado that he would fly the city. Peter, through their importunity at length persuaded, prepared himself to avoid. But, coming to the gate, he saw the Lord Christ come to meet him, to whom he, worshipping, said, "Lord, whither dost Thou go?" To whom He answered and said, "I am come again to be crucified." By this, Peter, perceiving his suffering to be understood, returned into the city. Jerome saith that he was crucified, his head being down and his feet upward, himself so requiring, because he was (he said) unworthy to be crucified after the same form and manner as the Lord was.*

Paul – Considered the greatest apostle of all time, Paul was said to have lost his life for the gospel when soldiers came, led him out of the city and cut his head off with a sword.

Jude - Crucified

Bartholomew – Translated the book of Matthew into the language of India and worked to have it spread through the country. He was beaten at length and crucified.

Thomas – The one once noted for his doubt, Thomas preached in Parthi and India and pushed back the works of paganism in those areas. His life ended when he was thrust with a spear.

Luke – Known as the evangelist, Luke is credited for penning the gospel with his name and the book of Acts. It is said that he traveled with Paul. His life ended supposedly when he was hung on an olive tree.

Simon – Crucified

John – Known as the "beloved disciple," John founded the churches in Smyrna, Pergamos, Sardis, Philadelphia, Laodicea, and Thyatira. He was punished by being cast into a cauldron of burning oil, which he escaped miraculously without injury. He was later banished to the Isle of Patmos, where He was visited by the Lord Jesus and received what he wrote in Revelation. He was the only apostle to avoid a tragic and violent death.

Yet even with all of the tragedy and violent deaths, the church not only remained strong, but daily *increased*. It is a clear example for us to follow – especially for those who are willing to jump out and face their fears.

These examples are certainly extreme illustrations, but I use them to close this chapter by posing a question to you. If the apostles faced death without fear, think of what you could face in your life, without fear. Before you take this book and put it down, let me challenge you to do an exercise. Write the answers down to this question.

Imagine your life without fear. What kind of things would you do if your life was void of fear? What would you spend your time doing if you had no fear? What are you holding back from doing as a result of fear? What would your life be like if you had no fear (even of death) in it?

I found this to be a powerful exercise because it showed me the many things I have avoided because fear stood in my way. Yet it is so amazing and freeing when we decide that we are no longer going to be driven by fear in any way in our lives and we refuse to make decisions based on it.

[1] *Fox's Book of Martyrs: A History of the Lives, Sufferings, and Deaths of the Early Christian and Protestant Martyrs*, written by John Foxe and edited by William Byron Forbush. http://www.ccel.org/f/foxe/martyrs/home.html

Chapter 21

Facing Your Fears

. . . and having done all, to stand. Stand therefore . . .
Ephesians 6:13b-14a

I feel led to close this book by brining a final challenge as you cast out the work of fear in your life. I must tell you some good news and some bad news. The bad news is that fear will always try to work in your life. The good news is that you have the weapons available to not only face fear, but to walk all over it when it tries to work. Your discernment can be elevated to a greater level as you learn to do battle and overcome. *As you gain victory in specific fears, you will gain the ability to walk in higher realms of authority in God's kingdom.*

As you seek to gain freedom, I must tell you this: *True victory over fear really only takes shape when you face your fears.* You have to take a step of faith and face those areas that used to keep you completely bound. The only way to really shut the mouth of fear and bring silence to its torment is to face it and make a display of fear's lies by proving there is nothing to be afraid of.

Remember, at the core of battling fear's projections, it is simply a bunch of smoke, mirrors and fireworks. Fear is not true reality. The majority of things that we fear don't even happen anyway. And with God, you will be ok. As you realize this within, you will grow in your walk.

At some point you will need to make a decision to start moving *towards* the things you used to move *away* from in fear. Some of you are waiting on God, but in reality God is waiting on you to stand in faith and see Him meet you as you take a risk. Those who have agoraphobia, will eventually need to get in the car and go with a friend to the mall. Those who struggle with a fear of poverty need to release their financial fears and make new decisions. For those who struggle with a fear of rejection, they will need to face their fears and open up to someone--taking the risk of transparency.

In the parable of the talents, the one who was given one talent became afraid and hid it in the ground, rather than investing it and using it to bring a return. Jesus called this person a wicked and lazy servant, all because he did not step out and use his talent. In fact, his talent was taken and given to the others who were using theirs. This is a tragic story when there could have been so much harvest and blessing.

Do not bury in fear what God wants you to use and bless others with. Face the fear and step into victory. I know the number one fear of Americans is public speaking. I believe that at some point, we are all going to need to break that fear so we can share our testimony and the Word of the Lord with love and grace. Do not let the enemy convince you that you are just shy and have nothing to offer. I encourage you to refuse to allow fear to push your talents and gifts down. The world needs your ministry and desperately needs what you have to offer them.

Defeating fear comes when we take our attention off ourselves and we minister to others. Doing this causes *boldness* and *love* to be stirred up. Fear focuses on "what is going on with me? What is going to happen to me? Will I be preserved?" Boldness and love thinks about others and how to bring blessing and healing to them. Serving the body and reaching out gets your mind off of all your phobias and focuses your heart on the harvest and the Kingdom of God. That is how God wants us to think. He desires to see us take risks and make great strides for the kingdom of God as we walk in faith.

My prayer for you as you go forth is that you face your fears, knowing that your Father has your back and will do great things in your life as you trust in Him!

Go in faith! Be yourself! Be free in love!

Appendix 1: A Relationship with God

God loves you very dearly and has an amazing purpose and plan for your life.

We love Him because He first loved us.
1 John 4:19

For God so loved the world that He gave His only begotten Son, that whoever believes in Him should not perish but have everlasting life.
John 3:16

The thief does not come except to steal, and to kill, and to destroy. I have come that they may have life, and that they may have it more abundantly.
John 10:10

Because of sin, man is separated from God and cannot know and experience His love and purposes.

for all have sinned and fall short of the glory of God,
Romans 3:23

For the wages of sin is death, but the gift of God is eternal life in Christ Jesus our Lord.
Romans 6:23

Jesus Christ came to earth and died on the cross for our sins. He rose from the dead and is the only way to a relationship with God. Through Jesus, we can know God's love and purpose for our life.

But God demonstrates His own love toward us, in that while we were still sinners, Christ died for us.
Romans 5:8

Jesus said to him, "I am the way, the truth, and the life. No one comes to the Father except through Me.
John 14:6

Jesus invites us to open up to God and have an intimate relationship with Him.

Behold, I stand at the door and knock. If anyone hears My voice and opens the door, I will come in to him and dine with him, and he with Me.
Revelation 3:20

Our responsibility is to believe and receive Jesus Christ as our Savior and Lord.

But as many as received Him, to them He gave the right to become children of God, to those who believe in His name.
John1:12

When we receive Christ, we do so by faith, believing in what He did on the cross, not on our own ability or works.

For by grace you have been saved through faith, and that not of yourselves; it is the gift of God, not of works, lest anyone should boast.
Ephesians 2:8-9 (NKJV)

You can receive Christ now by faith and enter into a new relationship with God through prayer.

If you confess with your mouth the Lord Jesus and believe in your heart that God has raised Him from the dead, you will be saved.
For with the heart one believes unto righteousness, and with the mouth confession is made unto salvation.
For the Scripture says, "Whoever believes on Him will not be put to shame."
For there is no distinction between Jew and Greek, for the same Lord over all is rich to all who call upon Him.
For "whoever calls on the name of the Lord shall be saved."
Romans 10:9-13

Here is a suggested prayer:

"Jesus, I recognize my need for You. I thank You for dying on the cross for my sins, and I open my heart to You right now. I receive your forgiveness for my sins and I thank You for giving me eternal life. I receive You as my Savior and Lord. I invite You to come in and take control of my life. Show me Your love and lead me to become the person You want me to be."

If this prayer echoes the desire of your heart, I invite you to pray it right now and Jesus will come into your life, as He promised.

Scriptures used in this appendix are from the New King James Version of the Bible

Appendix 2: Practical Helps

Here are some practical tips in dealing with fear that can be helpful when you are in the trenches and in the line of fire where fear's missiles are coming at you. When you feel completely overwhelmed by stress, anxiety or worry, here are some tips that go along with the teaching in this book that can help carry you through. Remember, not every time anxiety, panic and worry kick up is a spirit right there. It may be the result of programmed areas of the mind that have not been renewed yet. Remember that renewing the mind takes time. It also may be the result of your body not having enough rest or care.

In the meantime, here are some tips when you feel overwhelmed.

1. If you can, take a moment to get alone. If you work in an office, go into the bathroom or outside and take some deep breaths to allow your body to settle for a moment. Then begin to repent for whatever fear you are agreeing with and remove the fear that is knocking at your door. Tell it to leave until you sense that you are getting some relief, or until you have to go back inside. This is something I practice continually.

2. Remember that the area that is bringing up fear is an area that you have not been perfected in love. Seek Father God in your own way to receive a greater measure of His love.

3. You do not have to make a panic decision right now. Also, do not make major decisions during this time unless it is a decision to go all out against fear. Give it time because this will pass. Allow yourself time to renew your mind and break poor thinking patterns.

4. Begin right away speaking against the spirit of fear and tell it to leave. Name it specifically and take authority against it. If you are in a public setting or sitting across from the person that fear is using against you, speak under your breath.

5. Speak the Word of God to yourself out loud. Encourage yourself in the Lord, even if you are having a hard time believing what you are saying. Sometimes you need to say it until it sinks into your heart and mind.

6. Ask yourself, am I doing too much? Have I allowed myself to get into drivenness to try and do too much in too little time? Am I putting too much pressure on myself? If the answer is "yes," then give yourself a break and cut back a little bit.

7. Take some time to talk to someone about what is causing you to feel fearful. Speak with someone who understands spiritual matters and can help you walk out of your fear. Sometimes simply talking it out can bring great help.

8. Take a moment to listen to your favorite worship song that speaks of God greatness or His love for you. His presence has a way of changing our perspective.

9. Exercise. Exercise. Exercise. It helps your body to release endorphins and regulate hormones that bring you to homeostasis.

10. Eat a well balanced diet. My advice, eat everything in moderation and do not use food as a way to calm your fears. Eat properly to take care of the temple which houses the Spirit of God.

11. Do not quit. Whatever happens, do not ever, ever, ever quit. Do not ever let the enemy push you to quit. Greater is He who is in you than he who is in the world. Execute it!

12. Make an ongoing declaration that you will no longer run away but will face those things which you fear. With God on your side, victory is on its way! Join me in the cry that says, "I Will Not Fear!"

THM **TURNING HEARTS MINISTRIES**

For more information regarding
Mark DeJesus and Turning Hearts Ministries:

www.markdejesus.com